THE SHIPS OF ELLIS ISLAND

William H. Miller

Front Cover: Holland America Line's *Nieuw Amsterdam* arriving in New York's Upper Bay, in a painting by Stephen Card.

First published 2016

Amberley Publishing
The Hill, Stroud
Gloucestershire, GL5 4EP

www.amberley-books.com

Copyright © William H. Miller, 2016

The right of William H. Miller to be identified as the Author of this work has been asserted in accordance with the Copyrights, Designs and Patents Act 1988.

ISBN 978 1 4456 5162 0 (print)
ISBN 978 1 4456 5163 7 (ebook)

All rights reserved. No part of this book may be reprinted or reproduced or utilised in any form or by any electronic, mechanical or other means, now known or hereafter invented, including photocopying and recording, or in any information storage or retrieval system, without the permission in writing from the Publishers.

British Library Cataloguing in Publication Data.
A catalogue record for this book is available from the British Library.

Typeset in 10pt on 12pt Sabon LT Std.
Typesetting by Amberley Publishing.
Printed in the UK.

*To all those souls that crossed the great Atlantic
and landed at Ellis Island
– those humble and huddled masses.*

CONTENTS

Acknowledgments	7
Foreword	9
Introduction	11
The Ships of Ellis Island	17
Bibliography	128

ACKNOWLEDGMENTS

Many hands have assisted in this project. The author is particularly grateful to Amberley Publishing and especially to Louis Archard for taking on this project. It has been long overdue and now, even this modified version, it will at last happily see the light of day.

Initially, back in 1999, this was the biggest research project that I had ever done on the subject of passenger ships. In all, nearly 1,000 ship names – all of them from the official lists at Ellis Island – were given to me, to research and document. Some ships were immediately known to me; others, and sometimes the shipowners themselves, were vague. Recording some of the ships was the greatest, most time-consuming phase of the project. In the course of ten months, until June 2000, I pulled stacks of books from my own library shelves, used books loaned by others and then called upon maritime friends as far off as London, Hamburg, Trieste and Tokyo. As always, I have been most fortunate to have been met with great support and generosity. Consequently, there are many hands that I must thank.

Foremost appreciation to Larry Ballante and the Statue of Liberty-Ellis Island Museum for creating 'The Ships of Ellis Island' in the first place. Then thanks to Amberley Publishing and Louis Archard for reviving the idea and suggesting the modified, possibly more realistic version of some 100 ships. Very special thanks to Duncan Haws, a friend and fellow maritime author, who offered perhaps the greatest help with research. He not only provided the historical and statistical information for many of the more obscure and remote ships, but – with his splendid artistic skill – specially created drawings of many of the ships lacking a photographic portrait. Then there was the great help from the staff at the Peabody Essex Museum in Salem, Massachusetts. Their photo archives are among the finest anywhere.

Great thanks to Michael Hadgis for his technical assistance and to the late Alex Duncan, Richard Faber, Andreas Hernandez, Anthony La Forgia, the late Frank Pichardo and Albert Wilhelmi. Further assistance came from some of the very finest maritime historians and authors: the late Frank Braynard, Anthony Cooke, Luis Miguel Correia, the late Laurence Dunn, Maurizio Eliseo, Arnold Kludas, Hisashi Noma and Paolo Piccione.

Other photographic help came from Michael Cassar, John Clarkson, the late F. W. Hawks, D. H. Johnson, Eric Johnson, Tom Rayner, Gordon Turner, V. H. Young and L. A. Sawyer. Further help came from the Cunard Line, French Line, Klaus Feust at the German Ship Museum, H. J. Capell and Hapag-Lloyd, and the Real Photographs

Company. Special thanks to dear friends such as Tom Cassidy, the late Hayward Cirker, Tom Greene, Charles Howland, Peter Ising, Norman Knebel, Victor Marinelli, Tim Noble, Marie Radigan, the late Der Scutt, the late Michael Shernoff and Margaret Singagliese. And last but by no means least, great thanks to my dear friend and business partner, the late Abe Michaelson, for his unending support and assistance.

FOREWORD

I know of some of Bill Miller's books about the great ocean liners, those 'floating palaces'. He has so successively told us, reminded us and, through fascinating photos, documented the style, the beauty, the great ambience of those great ocean liners. There were the period photos and his well-worded descriptions of the grand lounges and salons, the luxurious quarters, the movie stars posing on deck – even the dogs pampered in top-deck kennels. It was a glorious, very glamorous age.

But this book by Bill is different. It documents the ships that provided transport – and transport in far less glamorous and grand accommodation. These are the ships, some of the ships, which carried immigrants. They delivered the 'huddled masses', those poor and often very poor people that often so bravely left the Old World to journey to the New. These are the ships that had large, if very basic and sometimes even quite primitive, accommodation in Third Class and Steerage. Herein, Bill documents some of these ships, a special breed of Atlantic liners, which helped to build twentieth-century America. They landed millions – and mostly for entry through Ellis Island. They came from northern Norway, from deepest Russia, from the smallest Greek village and from the deserts of Egypt. It was, in many ways, an unending process.

Myself, I feel personally connected to this Bill Miller book. My own grandfather came through Ellis Island, arriving from Sicily onboard the *Conte Verde*. That was in 1924. He came in Steerage, with about fifty other men in a lower-deck dormitory, arriving with little more than five dollars in his pocket and breaking into tears as he first saw the Statue of Liberty. He told me of the rough seas, the illness among many other passengers, his own feelings of uncertainty and facing the unknown. He arrived on a Monday morning, passed through Ellis Island and – focused and determined – began working in a leather factory at 5.30 a.m. on Tuesday morning. He had settled in Hoboken, my hometown as well as Bill's.

I am grateful to Bill for creating this book. Just as for myself with my grandfather, documenting and listing these ships creates a link to past generations, to relatives, to their bravery, their fortitude, their determination. Thank you, Bill, for giving us *The Ships of Ellis Island*.

John Minervini
New Jersey USA
Fall 2015

INTRODUCTION

I've written a great deal and in many books, over ninety in all, about the great ocean liners – ships such as the *Queen Mary*, the *United States* and the *Normandie*. These were 'ships of luxury'. But in this latest title, I write of the 'ships of destiny'. The ships of Ellis Island transported, well into the millions, those souls – the infamous 'huddled masses' – across the vast Atlantic from the Old World to the New. Perhaps no group of ships has ever performed such a vast task. They participated in the greatest flow of immigration the world has ever seen. They sailed in a twenty-two-year period between 1892 and 1924, from when Ellis Island, the immigration station in New York harbour, first opened until the start of the US government's vastly curtailed immigration quotas. It was this great flow of humble, poor, but driven peoples that created such a special part of history, in particular the building of America as it is today. It created the great 'melting pot' of peoples. Altogether, there are 818 different ships on the official Ellis Island manifests. However, that number is far too great for any ordinary-sized book. Instead, this book will look at 100 ships – famous, well remembered, but also varied. Consequently, the list ranges from the likes of such floating palaces as the *Aquitania*, *Leviathan* and *Majestic* to far smaller, barely known ships as the *Batavia*, *Belvedere* and *San Guglielmo*.

As each of these ships included in these pages arrived in the waters of New York's Lower Bay, they delivered the latest immigrants – the legendary Steerage passengers – to Ellis Island. They were tendered from anchored ships to early morning sessions with immigration officials and medical inspectors. It was often a tense experience, if not downright terrifying. Happily, 98 per cent were accepted – some 18 million in all. The nation's population grew and grew, and together these brave travellers brought a youthful United States into its own middle age. Almost suddenly, there were great numbers of Poles and Scandinavians about and along with the likes of the English, Irish, Dutch, Germans and the Spanish, Austro-Hungarians, Russians, Ukrainians, Greeks and Turks.

Europe was teeming with people on the eve of the twentieth century. Many of these people were poor; they had little economic opportunity. Others faced political and/or religious oppression. The New World was often their only hope, and so a voyage across the otherwise forbidding North Atlantic became a necessary and important part of the process, the immigrant experience. A ticket by sea might cost as little as $10 per person or as high as $20 or $25, depending upon the ship, the route and the length of voyage. On the Hamburg America Line, not only one

12   THE SHIPS OF ELLIS ISLAND

Left: The great symbol: The Statue of Liberty. (Author's Collection)

Opposite: Library of Congress.

THE SHIPS OF ELLIS ISLAND   13

14   THE SHIPS OF ELLIS ISLAND

New York harbour's Upper Bay. (Library of Congress)

of the biggest shipping lines but one of the best run, even in lower-deck, austere Steerage, seven days in a dormitory on the bottom passenger deck aboard their *Furst Bismarck* was advertised at $18 in 1900. People often sold every possession they had to raise the money for a railway ticket to the nearest seaport and then for the steamer tickets to America. Some used money sent by hardworking relatives already in America. They left their cities, towns and little villages and went to the terminals and the dock sides of Hamburg and Rotterdam, London and Queenstown (now Cobh), Genoa and Fiume (now Trieste), Piraeus and Odessa. They walked up gangways, laden with their limited, but total and often cherished, belongings onto ships belonging to North German Lloyd or the Scandinavian American Line, the Allan Line or Cunard Line, the La Veloce Line or the Greek National Line.

Once aboard, the immigrants settled into small, crowded cabins or, more often, dormitories. Activity, excitement and high anticipation filled the air. A great journey, perhaps the greatest journey of all for many of these Steerage passengers, was about to begin. Down below, crews prepared the ships. A sign of imminent departure was the thick, black smoke that belched from the funnel or funnels. Then the screeching steam whistle sounded. Soon the journey began.

The funnels of these ships were, by the way, a very important part of the economics of Steerage travel. Immigrants tended to select the ship for their voyage by viewing large posters at steamship offices, railway stations, post offices, hotels, village squares, even pubs. A theory among them evolved that a ship with more funnels was safer – two funnels being safer than a one-funnel ship, but three funnels even safer. Obviously, the few four-funnel liners were considered the safest. Every immigrant preferred to be on the safest ship for the inhibiting, very daunting journey across the often ferocious Atlantic. Later, at dock sides, however, many travellers were often surprised and even shocked to see what had been depicted as a mighty three-stacker was in fact not only a far smaller ship, but one with just one or two funnels. Expectedly, huge three- and four-stackers like the *Mauretania*, *Olympic* and *Imperator* were among the most successful ships, especially in the lucrative Third Class trade to America.

New York was of course America's chief port of entry, accounting for over 70 per cent of all immigrants. Ellis Island, built as a specialised immigrant station in the Upper Bay, opened on 1 January 1892. In the next twenty-two years, until the government's strict, much-reduced immigration quotas of 1924, over 12 million newcomers passed through the island's doors, waiting rooms and examining stations. 'It was the Plymouth Rock of its time,' said the writers of an extensive book titled *Ellis Island: An Illustrated History of the Immigrant Experience*. The year 1892 marked the beginning of America's greatest immigrant experience. Today, over 100 million Americans can trace at least some ancestry through Ellis Island.

The daily rate of incoming immigrants usually exceeded 5,000. 17 April 1907 was the busiest day on record, when 11,747 immigrants arrived and were processed. 1907 was also the island's busiest year, with over 1 million arrivals.

This is one of the largest number of ships I have covered in a single book. There were over 818 ships in all on the handwritten Ellis Island manifests made between 1892 and 1924, many of them quite remote, even obscure. I have limited it to approximately 100 ships, including some of the more famous and well known. Obviously, none remain. Most of the shipowners have long since left the business and so, quite often, records of ships have been difficult to come by. The general maritime historian and passenger ship enthusiast book markets have been largely linked to the big, better-known liners. The smaller ships, of which I have included a random few, are less well remembered but certainly interesting. Some ships made many voyages; others made as few as one or two. I have enjoyed researching them. Hopefully, this book will add to passenger ship history as well as the Ellis Island immigrant story.

Where available, each ship entry includes basic technical information: shipbuilder and year of completion; tonnage; length and width (overall length is normally given and is the measurement from tip to tip of the ship, but in some instances 'bp', between perpendiculars, length is shown and this is the distance from the fore side of the stem to the after side of the rudder post); the propulsion machinery and the number of propellers (screws); the service speed, and the passenger capacity (usually shown by class as well). Subsequent information is a synopsis of the ship's career: route, former owners and names, and then final disposition.

In 2000, I met John Stromberg on a luxury cruise in the Mediterranean. He was very interested in passenger ships and in particular the immigrant process to America. If I were to write a book on the ships of Ellis Island, he would be among the first to purchase one. 'Back in 1901, my father wanted to immigrate to America from Germany,' he told me,

> But he didn't have enough money, not even enough money for a passport and the other necessary documents for my mother and himself. So he took a job on the *Deutschland* as a coal stoker earning $3 a month. The *Deutschland* was then the fastest liner in the world. He made six roundtrips aboard her, to New York (Hoboken) and back, and finally saved enough money to make the one-way trip to New York, to the New World, as a Third Class passenger. He and my father both passed through Ellis Island. They became citizens, proud and hardworking Americans. My father and mother went back to Germany for a visit, to see family, in the 1920s. Then they could afford improved Tourist Class quarters on another German liner, the *Reliance*. They went again about ten years later, in the late 1930s, but then in Second Class on a very fine super liner, the *Europa*. Their last trip was in 1960, almost sixty years since their first voyage in Steerage. Then they sailed in First Class on the luxurious *Bremen*. Their travels reflect, especially to me, the decades of transatlantic passenger ship history as well as their personal ascent from Steerage to Second Class and finally into First Class. It is a reflection of sorts of the American success process. I will look forward to your book. It will be a link to my parents.

Hopefully, this book will be useful to others as well. The American immigrant story is a remarkable one – and the resurrection and creation of Ellis Island as a fine, very popular museum is testament to that story. These ships were an important part of the overall story. In a way, they now sail once again in the pages of this book. Myself, I can almost see them in New York's Lower Bay, pausing as they offload their Third Class/Steerage passengers into tenders, ferries and other craft bound for Ellis Island.

Bill Miller
Secaucus, New Jersey
Summer 2015

THE SHIPS OF ELLIS ISLAND

Adriatic

Built at Harland & Wolff Ltd, Belfast, Northern Ireland, 1907. 24,541 gross tons; 726 feet long; 75 feet wide. Steam quadruple-expansion engines, twin screw. Service speed 17 knots. 2,825 passengers (425 First Class, 500 Second Class, 1,900 Steerage).
    Built for White Star Line, British flag. Liverpool–Queenstown–New York service. Broken up in Japan, 1935.

Albania

Built by Scott's Shipbuilding & Engineering Co., Greenock, Scotland, 1920. 12,768 gross tons; 539 feet long; 64 feet wide. Steam turbines, twin screw. Service speed 13 knots. 480 one-class passengers.
    Built for Cunard Line, British flag. Liverpool–Montreal and later Liverpool–Queenstown–New York service. Laid up 1925–30. Sold to Navigazione Libera Triestino, Italian flag, in 1930 and renamed *California*. Bombed and sunk by British aircraft off Sicily on 11 August 1941. Later refloated and scrapped.

Alaunia

Built by Scott's Shipbuilding & Engineering Co., Greenock, Scotland, 1913. 13,405 gross tons; 540 feet long; 64 feet wide. Steam quadruple-expansion engines, twin screw. Service speed 16 knots. 2,060 passengers (520 Second Class, 1,540 Third Class).
    Built for Cunard Line, British flag. Liverpool–Queenstown–Boston and later Liverpool–Queenstown–New York service. Mined and sank off the English coast on 19 October 1916; two lost.

Albert Ballin

Built by Blohm & Voss Shipbuilders, Hamburg, Germany, 1923. 20,815 gross tons; 627 feet long; 72 feet wide. Steam turbines, twin screw. Service speed 15½ knots. 1,551 passengers (251 First Class, 340 Second Class, 960 Third Class).
    Built for Hamburg America Line, German flag. Hamburg–Southampton–Cherbourg–New York service. Extensively rebuilt in 1930 and in 1934 (extended to 677 feet in length). Renamed *Hansa*

Adriatic. (Alex Duncan)

Albania. (World Ship Society)

THE SHIPS OF ELLIS ISLAND   19

Above: Alaunia. (World Ship Society)

Right: Cunard Line poster. (Cunard Line)

20 THE SHIPS OF ELLIS ISLAND

Above: Albert Ballin. (Hamburg America Line)

Right: Hamburg America Line poster. (Hamburg America Line)

in 1935. Laid up at the start of the Second World War in September 1939. Later became a training ship for the German navy. Mined off Warnemunde on 6 March 1945. Salvaged by the Soviet government in 1949 and rebuilt. Renamed *Sovetsky Sojus*, the largest passenger ship under the Soviet flag. Vladivostock–Far East service. Renamed *Soyuz* in 1980. Scrapped in 1981.

Alice/Asia

Built by Russell & Co., Port Glasgow, Scotland, 1907. 6,122 gross tons; 415 (bp) feet long; 49 feet wide. Steam triple-expansion engines, twin screw. Service speed 15 knots. 1,625 passengers (50 First Class, 75 Second Class, 1,500 Third Class).

Built for Austro-Americana Line (Unione Austriaca), Austrian flag. Trieste–Dalmatian ports–Patras–Palermo–Algiers–Almeria–New York service. Seized by the Brazilian government during the First World War, in 1917; renamed *Asia*. Ceded to France as reparations in 1919; later sold to Fabre Line, French flag; continued as *Asia*. Marseilles–New York (occasionally extended to include Piraeus, Istanbul, Beirut, Jaffa and Alexandria) service 1920–29. Destroyed by fire while carrying pilgrims to Mecca on 21 May 1930.

Amerika/America

Built by Harland & Wolff Ltd, Belfast, Northern Ireland, 1905. 22,225 gross tons; 700 feet long; 74 feet wide. Steam quadruple-expansion engines, twin screw. Service speed 17½ knots. 2,662 passengers (420 First Class, 254 Second Class, 223 Third Class, 1,765 Steerage).

Built for Hamburg America Line, German flag. The largest ship afloat 1905/06. Hamburg–Southampton–Cherbourg–New York service. Laid up at Boston at the outbreak of war in Europe in August 1914; later seized by the US government, becoming the troopship USS *America*. Resumed transatlantic passenger service in 1921, but for United States Lines, US flag, and as *America*. Laid up 1931–40. Rebuilt 1940/41 as the troopship USS *Edmund B. Alexander*. Laid up 1949–57; scrapped at Baltimore in 1958.

Andania

Built by Scott's Shipbuilding & Engineering Co., Greenock, Scotland, 1913. 13,405 gross tons; 540 feet long; 64 feet wide. Steam quadruple-expansion engines, twin screw. Service speed 16 knots. 2,060 passengers (520 Second Class, 1,540 Third Class).

Built for Cunard Line, British flag. Liverpool–Queenstown–Boston and later Liverpool–Queenstown–New York service. Torpedoed and sunk by a German submarine off the Irish coast on 27 January 1918; seven lost.

Antonia

Built by Vickers-Armstrong Ltd, Barrow-in-Furness, England, 1921. 13,867 gross tons; 540 feet long; 65 feet wide. Steam turbines, twin screw. Service speed 15 knots. 1,700 passengers (500 cabin class, 1,200 Third Class).

Built for Cunard Line, British flag. Liverpool–Montreal and Liverpool–Queenstown–New York service. British troopship 1940–42. Sold to the British Admiralty in 1942 and rebuilt as the repair ship HMS *Wayland*. Scrapped in Scotland 1948.

Asia. (Alex Duncan)

America. (United States Lines)

Aquitania

Built by John Brown & Co. Ltd, Clydebank, Scotland, 1914. 45,647 gross tons; 901 feet long; 97 feet wide. Steam turbines, quadruple screw. Service speed 23 knots. 3,230 passengers (618 First Class, 614 Second Class, 1,998 Third Class).

   Built for Cunard Line, British flag. Southampton–Cherbourg–New York service. Served as an auxiliary cruiser and then as a troopship during First World War, 1914–18. Resumed Cunard service 1919–39. Used as a troopship, 1939–48. Resumed Cunard transatlantic service, Southampton–Halifax, 1948–49. Last four-funnel liner. Broken up in Scotland in 1950.

Arabic

Built by Harland & Wolff Ltd, Belfast, Northern Ireland, 1903. 15,801 gross tons; 616 feet long; 65 feet wide. Steam quadruple-expansion engines, twin screw. Service speed 16 knots. Over 2,000 passengers (exact numbers not known for First Class and Steerage).

   Intended to be the *Minnewaska* for the Atlantic Transport Line, British flag, but never completed as such. Sold to White Star Line, British flag, and completed as *Arabic*. Liverpool–Queenstown–Boston or Liverpool–Queenstown–New York service. Sunk by a German U-boat off southern Ireland, 19 August 1915; forty-four lost.

Araguaya

Built by Workman, Clark & Co., Belfast, Northern Ireland, 1906. 10,537 gross tons; 532 feet long; 61 feet wide. Steam quadruple-expansion engines, twin screw. Service speed 16 knots. 1,185 passengers (285 First Class, 100 Second Class, 800 Third Class).

   Built for Royal Mail Lines, British flag. Southampton–East Coast of South America service. Hamburg–Southampton–Cherbourg–New York service 1921–26. Resumed South American service afterward. Sold to Yugoslav Lloyd, Yugoslav flag, in 1930 and renamed *Kraljica Marija*. Mediterranean service and cruising. Sold to French government in 1940; renamed *Savoie*. Sunk off Casablanca on 8 November 1942.

Armenia

Built by Palmer's Shipbuilding & Iron Co., Jarrow-on-Tyne, England, 1896. 5,458 gross tons; 399 (bp) feet long; 50 feet wide. Steam quadruple-expansion engines, twin screw. Service speed 13 knots. 1,130 passengers (20 First Class, 1,100 Third Class).

   Built for Hamburg America Line, German flag. Hamburg–New York service; Hamburg–Baltimore service. Laid up at Baltimore during the First World War, 1914–17. Seized by the US government in 1917 and refitted as transport USS *Armenia*. Scrapped at Baltimore 1924.

Ascania

Built by Swan, Hunter & Wigham Richardson Ltd, Wallsend-on-Tyne, England, 1911. 9,111 gross tons; 482 feet long; 56 feet wide. Steam triple-expansion engines, twin screw. Service speed 13 knots. 1,700 passengers (200 Second Class, 1,500 Third Class).

   Ordered as *Gerona* for Thomson Line, British flag, but sold to Cunard Line, also British flag, while under construction and renamed *Ascania*. London–Southampton–Montreal and London–Southampton–New York service. Wrecked off Newfoundland on 13 June 1918.

Above and right: Aquitania. (Cunard Line)

Araguaya. (Royal Mail Lines)

Armenia. (Peabody Essex Museum)

THE SHIPS OF ELLIS ISLAND 27

Ascania. (Peabody Essex Museum)

Ausonia

Built by Swan, Hunter & Wigham Richardson Ltd, Wallsend-on-Tyne, England, 1909. 8,153 gross tons; 450 (bp) feet long; 54 feet wide. Steam triple-expansion engines, single screw. Service speed 13 knots. 1,090 passengers (90 Second Class, 1,000 Third Class).

Launched as *Tortona* for Thomson Line, British flag, but then sold to Cunard Line, also British flag, and completed as *Ausonia*. London–Montreal and later Glasgow–New York service. Torpedoed and sunk by a German submarine in the Irish Sea on 30 May 1918; forty-four lost.

Balmoral Castle

Built by Fairfield Shipbuilding & Engineering Co., Glasgow, Scotland, 1910. 13,361 gross tons; 590 feet long; 64 feet wide. Steam quadruple-expansion engines, twin screw. Service speed 17 knots. 810 passengers (320 First Class, 220 Second Class, 270 Third Class).

Built for Union-Castle Line, British flag. Southampton–Cape Town–Durban service. Used as a troopship during the First World War, 1917–18. Made some Southampton–New York voyages for Cunard in 1919. Resumed South African service 1919–39. Scrapped 1939.

Baltic

Built by Harland & Wolff Ltd, Belfast, Northern Ireland, 1904. 23,884 gross tons; 726 feet long; 75 feet wide. Steam quadruple-expansion engines, twin screw. Service speed 16 knots. 2,875 passengers (425 First Class, 450 Second Class, 2,000 Steerage).

Built for White Star Line, British flag. Liverpool–Queenstown–New York service. Largest ship afloat 1904–05. Used as a troopship during the First World War, 1914–18. Scrapped in Japan 1933.

Batavia

Built by Blohm & Voss Shipbuilders, Hamburg, Germany, 1899. 10,178 gross tons; 517 feet long; 62 feet wide. Steam quadruple-expansion engines, twin screw. Service speed 12½ knots. 2,700 passengers (300 Second Class, 2,400 Steerage).

Built for Hamburg America Line, German flag. Genoa–Naples–New York service. Also Hamburg–Baltimore and Hamburg–Boston services. Sold to Union Austriaca, Austrian flag, and renamed *Polonia* in April 1913 for short-lived Trieste–Quebec City–Montreal service. Resold to Hamburg America Line, German flag, in August 1913 and reverted to original name. Laid up at Hamburg in August 1914 owing to the outbreak of the First World War. Briefly used in 1917 as the German navy transport *Batavia 7*. Transferred to the French government in 1919; operated by Messageries Maritimes on Marseilles–Far East service as *Batavia*. Scrapped 1924.

Belgenland

Built by Harland & Wolff Ltd, Belfast, Northern Ireland, 1914–17. 24,578 gross tons; 697 feet long; 78 feet wide. Steam triple-expansion engines, triple screw. Service speed 17 knots. 2,600 passengers (500 First Class, 600 Second Class, 1,500 Third Class).

Launched in 1914, but remained incomplete owing to the First World War. Completed in 1917, but as the cargo ship *Belgic* for White

Star Line, British flag. Rebuilt as a passenger ship 1922/23; renamed *Belgenland* for Red Star Line, Belgian flag. Antwerp–Southampton/London–New York service. Often used as a cruise ship. Laid up 1933–35. Sold to Panama Pacific Line, US flag, in 1935; renamed *Columbia*. Used only for cruising. Scrapped in Scotland in 1936.

Belgravia

Built by Blohm & Voss Shipbuilders, Hamburg, Germany, 1899. 10,155 gross tons; 516 feet long; 62 feet wide. Steam quadruple-expansion engines, twin screw. Service speed 12½ knots. 2,700 passengers (300 Second Class, 2,400 Steerage).

Built for Hamburg America Line, German flag. Hamburg–New York and Genoa–Naples–New York services as well as Hamburg–Baltimore service. Sold to the Russian Navy, Russian flag, in 1905 and refitted as transport *Riga*. Transferred to the Black Sea Steamship Company, also Russian, in 1906. Transferred to Sovtorgflot, also Russian, in 1920 and renamed *Transbalt*. Used as a hospital ship until 1923. Accidentally torpedoed on 13 June 1945 by a US submarine after having been misidentified as a Japanese freighter.

Belvedere

Built by Cantieri Navali Triestino, Monfalcone, Italy, 1913. 7,420 gross tons; 437 feet long; 51 feet wide. Steam triple-expansion engines, single screw. Service speed 13 knots. 1,544 passengers (144 Cabin Class, 1,400 Third Class).

Built for Austro-Americana Line (Unione Austriaca), Austrian flag. Trieste–South America service and later Trieste–New York service.

Sold to Cosulich Line, Italian flag, in 1919. Trieste–Dalmatian ports–Patras–Palermo–Algiers–Almeria–New York service. Seized by the US government during the Second World War, in 1941, and renamed USS *Audacious*. Scuttled in order to form a breakwater for Allied invasion forces off the Normandy coast in June 1944.

Bergensfjord

Built by Cammell Laird & Co., Birkenhead, England, 1913. 11,013 gross tons; 530 feet long; 61 feet wide. Steam quadruple-expansion engines, twin screw. Service speed 15 knots. 1,200 passengers (100 First Class, 250 Second Class, 850 Third Class).

Built for the Norwegian America Line, Norwegian flag. Oslo–Kristiansand–Stavanger–Bergen–New York service. Used as a troopship during the Second World War, 1940–46. Sold to Home Lines, Panamanian flag, in 1946 and renamed *Argentina*. Mediterranean–South America and Mediterranean–New York services. Sold to Zim Lines, Israeli flag, in 1953; renamed *Jerusalem*. Further Mediterranean–New York service. Renamed *Aliya* in 1957. Laid up 1958/59. Scrapped in Italy 1959.

Brasile

Built by Officine e Cantieri Liguri-Anconetani, Ancona, Italy, 1905. 5,026 gross tons; 394 (bp) feet long; 47 feet wide. Steam triple-expansion engines, twin screw. Service speed 14½ knots. 1,108 passengers (58 First Class, 56 Second Class, 994 Third Class).

Built for La Veloce Line, Italian flag. Genoa–Naples–New York service. Sold to the French Line, French flag, in 1912 and renamed *Venezuela*. Ran aground and later sank at Casablanca in 1920.

Ausonia. (Peabody Essex Museum)

Balmoral Castle. (Alex Duncan)

THE SHIPS OF ELLIS ISLAND 31

Baltic. (White Star Line)

Batavia. (Peabody Essex Museum)

32   THE SHIPS OF ELLIS ISLAND

Above: Belgravia. (Peabody Essex Museum)

Left: Belgenland. (Red Star Line)

Belvedere. (Peabody Essex Museum)

Bergensfjord. (Author's Collection)

Brasile. (Peabody Essex Museum)

Campania

Built by Fairfield Shipbuilding & Engineering Co., Glasgow, Scotland, 1893. 12,950 gross tons; 622 feet long; 65 feet wide. Steam triple-expansion engines, twin screw. Service speed 21 knots. 2,000 passengers (600 First Class, 400 Second Class, 1,000 Steerage).
    Built for Cunard Line, British flag. Liverpool–Queenstown–New York service. Sold for scrap in 1914, but then resold to British Admiralty and rebuilt as the aircraft carrier HMS *Campania*. Sunk following a collision in the Firth of Forth in Scotland on 5 November 1918.

Carmania

Built by John Brown & Co. Ltd, Clydebank, Scotland, 1905. 19,524 gross tons; 675 feet long; 72 feet wide. Steam turbines, triple screw. Service speed 18 knots. 2,650 passengers (300 First Class, 350 Second Class, 900 Third Class, 1,100 Steerage).
    Built for Cunard Line, British flag. Liverpool–Queenstown–New York service. Cunard's first steam turbine-driven liner (similar propulsion was used for most subsequent passenger ships). Served as an armed merchant cruiser then as a troopship during the First World War, 1914–18. Scrapped in Scotland in 1932.

Caronia

Built by John Brown & Co. Ltd, Clydebank, Scotland, 1905. 19,524 gross tons; 678 feet long; 72 feet wide. Steam quadruple-expansion engines, twin screw. Service speed 18 knots. 2,650 passengers (300 First Class, 350 Second Class, 900 Third Class, 1,100 Steerage).
    Built for Cunard Line, British flag. Liverpool–Queenstown–New York service. Served as an armed merchant cruiser and then as a troopship during the First World War, 1914–18. Scrapped in Japan 1933.

Carpathia

Built by Swan & Hunter Ltd, Newcastle, England, 1903. 13,603 gross tons; 558 feet long; 64 feet wide. Steam quadruple-expansion engines, twin screw. Service speed 14 knots. 1,704 passengers (204 First Class, 1,500 Third Class).
    Built for Cunard Line, British flag. Liverpool–Queenstown–New York as well as Fiume–Trieste–Venice–Palermo–New York services. The *Carpathia* rescued 705 survivors from the sunken *Titanic* on 15 April 1912 and brought them to New York. Torpedoed and sunk by a German submarine off the English coast on 17 July 1918; five lost.

Cedric

Built by Harland & Wolff Ltd, Belfast, Northern Ireland, 1902. 21,035 gross tons; 700 feet long; 75 feet wide. Steam quadruple-expansion engines, twin screw. Service speed 16 knots. 2,875 passengers (365 First Class, 160 Second Class, 2,350 Steerage).
    Built for White Star Line, British flag. Liverpool–Queenstown–New York service. Largest ship afloat 1903/04. Used as an auxiliary cruiser and then as a troopship during the First World War, 1914–18. Scrapped in Scotland in 1932.

36 THE SHIPS OF ELLIS ISLAND

Above and opposite: Campania. (Cunard Line)

THE SHIPS OF ELLIS ISLAND 37

CUNARD LINE

IN MID-ATLANTIC.

Above: Carmania. (Peabody Essex Museum)

Opposite: Caronia. (Cunard Line)

R.M.S. "Caronia" — Cunard Line

White Star Line.

Celtic

Built by Harland & Wolff Ltd, Belfast, Northern Ireland, 1901. 20,904 gross tons; 700 feet long; 75 feet wide. Steam quadruple-expansion engines, twin screw. Service speed 16 knots. 2,857 passengers (347 First Class, 160 Second Class, 2,350 Steerage).

Built for White Star Line, British flag. Liverpool–Queenstown–New York service. Largest ship afloat 1901/03. Used as an armed merchant cruiser and then as a troopship during the First World War, 1914–18. Stranded in Cobh harbour in December 1928; declared a total loss and gradually scrapped until 1933.

Cincinnati

Built by Schichau Shipyards, Danzig, Germany, 1909. 16,339 gross tons; 603 feet long; 63 feet wide. Steam quadruple-expansion engines, twin screw. Service speed 15½ knots. 2,827 passengers (246 First Class, 332 Second Class, 448 Third Class, 1,801 Steerage).

Built for Hamburg America Line, German flag. Hamburg–Boulogne–Southampton–Boston or New York service. Interned at Boston at the start of the First World War in August 1914. Seized by the US government and became troopship USS *Covington* in 1917. Torpedoed and sunk by a German U-boat in the North Atlantic on 1 July 1918.

City of New York/New York

Built by J. & G. Thomson, Glasgow, Scotland, 1888. 10,499 gross tons; 560 feet long; 60 feet wide. Steam triple-expansion engines, twin screw. Service speed 20 knots. 1,740 passengers (540 First Class, 200 Second Class, 1,000 Steerage).

Built for Inman Line, British flag. Liverpool/Southampton–New York service. World's fastest ship 1892–93. Sold to American Line, US flag, in 1893 and renamed *New York*. Liverpool/Southampton–New York service. Served briefly with the US Navy during the Spanish–American War in 1898 as the USS *Harvard*. Afterward reverted to American Line as the *New York*. Used as the armed merchant cruiser USS *Plattsburgh* during the First World War, 1917–19; then reverted to American Line as *New York* in 1919. Sold to Polish Navigation Company, US flag, for Danzig–New York service in 1921. Mediterranean–New York service in 1922. Scrapped at Genoa in 1923.

City of Paris/Paris (1889)/Philadelphia

Built by J. & G. Thomson, Glasgow, Scotland, 1889. 10,449 gross tons; 560 feet long; 63 feet wide. Steam triple-expansion engines, twin screw. Service speed 20 knots. 1,740 passengers (540 First Class, 200 Second Class, 1,000 Steerage).

Built for Inman Line, British flag. Liverpool/Southampton–New York service. World's fastest ship 1889–92. Sold to American Line, US flag, in 1893 and renamed *Paris*. Liverpool/Southampton–New York service. Served briefly for US Navy during Spanish–American war in 1898 as the auxiliary cruiser USS *Yale*; then reverted to American Line as *Paris*. Nearly lost after grounding off Cornwall on 21 May 1899; later refloated, repaired and renamed *Philadelphia*. Served with the US Navy during the First World War, 1917–19, as the armed transport USS *Harrisburg*. Reverted to American Line in 1919 and renamed *Philadelphia*. Laid up 1920–22. Sold to New York–Naples Steamship Company, US flag, in 1922 and to be used in New York–Naples service as *Philadelphia*. Mutiny on first voyage and ship laid up at Naples. Scrapped at Genoa in 1923.

Cleveland/King Alexander

Built by Blohm & Voss Shipbuilders, Hamburg, Germany, 1909. 16,960 gross tons; 607 feet long; 63 feet wide. Steam quadruple-expansion engines, twin screw. Service speed 15 ½ knots. 2,841 passengers (239 First Class, 224 Second Class, 496 Third Class, 1,882 Steerage).

Built for Hamburg America Line, German flag. Hamburg–Boulogne–Southampton–Boston or New York service. Laid up at Hamburg for duration of First World War, 1914–18. Seized by US government in 1919 and became troopship USS *Mobile*. Sold to Byron Steamship Company, British flag, in 1920; renamed *King Alexander* for Patras–Piraeus–New York service, sometimes extended to include Constantinople and Constanza or Smyrna, Beirut, Port Said and Alexandria. Sold to United America Lines, Panamanian flag, in 1923 and renamed *Cleveland*. Hamburg–Southampton–Cherbourg–New York service. Hamburg America Line brought their former ship in 1926, reverted to German flag and further Hamburg–Southampton–Cherbourg–New York service. Laid up 1931; scrapped at Hamburg 1933.

Columbus

Built by Schichau Shipyards, Danzig, Germany, 1924. 32,581 gross tons; 775 feet long; 83 feet wide. Steam turbines, twin screw. Service speed 23 knots. 1,725 passengers (479 Cabin Class, 644 Tourist Class, 602 Third Class).

Laid down as the *Hindenburg* for North German Lloyd, German flag, in 1914; construction then halted owing to the First World War. Not launched until 1922, renamed *Columbus* and finally completed in 1924. Bremerhaven–Southampton–Cherbourg–New York service. Deliberately set afire by her Nazi crew to avoid capture by a British warship in the western Atlantic on 19 December 1939.

Conte Rosso

Built by William Beardmore & Co. Ltd, Glasgow, Scotland, 1921. 18,017 gross tons; 591 feet long; 74 feet wide. Steam turbines, twin screw. Service speed 18½ knots. 2,366 passengers (208 First Class, 268 Second Class, 1,890 Third Class).

Built for Lloyd Sabaudo, Italian flag. Genoa–Naples–Palermo–New York service. Later used in Genoa–Rio de Janeiro–Buenos Aires service. Transferred to Italian Line in 1932 and reassigned to Italy–Far East service. Became a troopship for the Italian navy in 1940. Torpedoed by a British submarine while in the Mediterranean on 24 May 1941; over 800 perished.

Conte Verde

Built by William Beardmore & Company Limited, Glasgow, Scotland, 1923. 18,765 gross tons; 559 feet long; 74 feet wide. Steam turbines, twin screw. Service speed 18½ knots. 2,400 passengers (230 First Class, 290 Second Class, 1,880 Third Class).

Built for Lloyd Sabaudo, Italian flag. Genoa–Naples–Palermo–New York service. Later used in Genoa–Rio de Janeiro–Buenos Aires service. Transferred to Italian Line in 1932 and reassigned to Italy–Far East

Celtic. (Alex Duncan)

Above: City of New York. (Peabody Essex Museum)

Left: City of Paris. (Peabody Essex Museum)

THE SHIPS OF ELLIS ISLAND 45

Cleveland.
(Hamburg America Line)

Columbus.
(Hapag-Lloyd)

Conte Rosso. (Alex Duncan)

Conte Verde. (Richard Faber Collection)

service. Laid up at Shanghai at the start of the Second World War in 1940; later used as wartime prisoner exchange ship. Abandoned by crew and then deliberately sunk in September 1943; later salvaged by the Japanese, taken to Japan and restored as a troopship. Sunk during an American air raid in 1944; wreck raised 1949 and remains scrapped 1951.

Corcovado/Guglielmo Peirce

Built by Germania Werft (Krupp), Kiel, Germany, 1907. 8,512 gross tons; 448 (bp) feet long; 55 feet wide. Steam quadruple-expansion engines, twin screw. Service speed 12 knots. 1,650 passengers (50 First Class, 300 Second Class, 1,300 Third Class).

Built as *Corcovado* for Hamburg America Line, German flag. Hamburg–South America service. Laid up at Hamburg during the First World War. Sold to Sicula Americana Lines, Italian flag, in 1920; renamed *Guglielmo Peirce*. Palermo–Messina–Naples–New York service. Sold to Cosulich Line, also Italian flag, in 1926. Sold to Lloyd Sabaudo, also Italian flag, in 1927; renamed *Maria Cristina*. Sold to Companhia Colonial, Portugese flag, in 1930; renamed *Mouzinho*. Lisbon–Africa service. Scrapped in Italy 1954.

Crefeld

Built by A. G. Vulcan, Stettin, Germany, 1895. 3,829 gross tons; 355 (bp) feet long; 43 feet wide. Steam triple-expansion engines, twin screw. Service speed 12 knots. 1,045 passengers (32 Second Class, 1,013 Third Class).

Built for North German Lloyd, German flag. Bremerhaven–South America as well as Bremerhaven–Southampton–Cherbourg–New York services. Laid up in Spain during the First World War, 1914–18. Seized by the Spanish government in 1918; renamed *Espana No. 4*. Renamed *Teide* in 1925. Wrecked off West Africa on 10 June 1932.

Czar/Estonia

Built by Barclay Curle & Co. Ltd, Glasgow, Scotland, 1912. 6,503 gross tons; 426 (bp) feet long; 53 feet wide. Steam quadruple-expansion engines, twin screw. Service speed 16 knots. Information lacking on exact passenger capacity.

Built for Russian American Line, Russian flag. Libau–Copenhagen/Rotterdam–New York and later Archangel–New York service. Transferred to the British government after the Russian Revolution in 1917. Sold to Baltic American Line, Danish flag, in 1921; renamed *Estonia*. Libau–Danzig/Hamburg–New York service. Sold to Polish Transatlantic Shipping Company, Polish flag, in 1930; renamed *Pulaski*. Gdynia–Copenhagen–New York service. Gdynia–East Coast of South America service 1936–39. Used as a transport ship under British management during the Second World War, 1939–46. Transferred to the British Ministry of Transport, British flag, in 1946; renamed *Empire Penryn*. Scrapped 1949.

De Grasse

Built by Cammell Laird & Co., Birkenhead, England, 1924. 17,759 gross tons; 574 feet long; 71 feet wide. Steam turbines, twin screw. Service speed 16 knots. 2,111 passengers (399 Cabin Class, 1,712 Third Class).

Built for French Line, French flag. Le Havre–Southampton–New York and later Le Havre–Caribbean service. Scuttled at Bordeaux by French Resistance in July 1940, but later salvaged by Nazi invasion forces. Deliberately scuttled at Bordeaux by retreating Nazis in August 1944. Salvaged by the French in August 1945. Restored and resumed French Line service 1947–53. Sold to Canadian Pacific Steamships, British flag, in 1953; renamed *Empress of Australia*. Liverpool–Quebec City–Montreal service. Sold to Grimaldi-Siosa Lines, Italian flag, in 1956; renamed *Venezuela*. Italy–Caribbean service. Grounded near Cannes on 17 March 1962; so badly damaged that ship had to be scrapped in Italy.

Deutschland/Viktoria Luise/Hansa

Built by Vulkan Shipyards, Stettin, Germany, 1900. 16,502 gross tons; 684 feet long; 67 feet wide. Quadruple-expansion engines, twin screw. Service speed 22 knots. 2,050 passengers (450 First Class, 300 Second Class, 1,000 Steerage).

Built for Hamburg America Line, German flag. Bremerhaven–Southampton–Cherbourg–New York service. World's fastest passenger ship 1900–06. Mechanically troublesome; rebuilt 1910/11 and repainted in all-white as the all-First Class cruise ship *Viktoria Luise*. Laid up and unused in Germany during the First World War, but rebuilt as the immigrant ship *Hansa* in 1921. Bremerhaven–Plymouth–Cherbourg–New York service. Scrapped 1925.

Doric

Built by Harland & Wolff Ltd, Belfast, Northern Ireland, 1923. 16,484 gross tons; 601 feet long; 67 feet wide. Steam turbines, twin screw. Service speed 15 knots. 2,300 passengers (600 First Class, 1,700 Third Class).

Built for White Star Line, British flag. Liverpool–Quebec City–Montreal service; occasional Liverpool–Cobh–New York sailings. Beginning in 1930, she was mostly used for cruising. Following a collision with a French steamer off Portugal on 5 September 1935, *Doric* was badly damaged and, instead of repairs, was sold for scrap.

Drottningholm

Built by Alexander Stephen & Sons Ltd, Glasgow, Scotland, 1905. 11,182 gross tons; 538 feet long; 60 feet wide. Steam turbines, triple screw. Service speed 18 knots. 1,712 passengers (426 First Class, 286 Second Class, 1,000 Third Class).

Built as *Virginian* for Allan Line, British flag. England–Canada service. Transferred to Canadian Pacific Steamships, also British flag, in 1917. Sold to Swedish American Line, Swedish flag, in 1920 and renamed *Drottningholm*. Gothenburg–Copenhagen–New York service. During the Second World War she was used as an international exchange ship, 1940–45. Resumed Swedish American service 1946–48. Sold to Home Lines, Panamanian flag, in 1948; renamed *Brasil*. Mediterranean–South America and Mediterranean–New York service. Renamed *Homeland* in 1951. Hamburg–Southampton–Cherbourg–Halifax–New York service. Scrapped in Italy 1955.

Duilio

Built by Ansaldo Shipyards, Genoa, Italy, 1916–23. 24,281 gross tons; 635 feet long; 76 feet wide. Steam turbines, quadruple screw. Service

THE SHIPS OF ELLIS ISLAND 49

Corcovado. (German Ship Museum)

Crefeld. (Peabody Essex Museum)

Above: Czar. (Alex Duncan)

Left: De Grasse. (Alex Duncan)

THE SHIPS OF ELLIS ISLAND 51

Doric. (World Ship Society)

Drottningholm. (Alex Duncan)

speed 19 knots. 1,550 passengers (280 First Class, 670 Second Class, 600 Third Class).

Built for Navigazione Generale Italiana, Italian flag. Genoa–Naples–Palermo–New York service; Genoa–South America service after 1928. Transferred to Italian Line in 1932. Italy–South Africa service 1933–40. Transferred to Lloyd Triestino, Italian flag, in 1937. Laid up 1940–42. Used by International Red Cross as an evacuation ship in 1942; sunk during an Allied air raid on Trieste 10 July 1944. Wreckage raised and then scrapped in 1948.

Florida

Built by Societa Escerizio Bacini, Riva Trigoso, Italy, 1905. 5,018 gross tons; 381 (bp) feet long; 47 feet wide. Steam triple-expansion engines, twin screw. Service speed 14 knots. 1,625 passengers (25 First Class, 1,600 Third Class).

Built for Lloyd Italiano, Italian flag. Genoa–New York service. Sold to Ligure Brasiliana, Italian flag, in 1911; renamed *Cavour*. Sunk following a collision off Italy on 12 December 1917.

France

Built by Chantiers de Penhoet, St Nazaire, France, 1912. 23,666 gross tons; 713 feet long; 75 feet wide. Steam turbines, quadruple screw. Service speed 24 knots. 2,026 passengers (534 First Class, 442 Second Class, 250 Third Class, 800 Steerage).

Built for French Line, French flag. Le Havre–Plymouth–New York service. Used as an auxiliary cruiser, hospital ship and troopship during the First World War, 1914–18. Resumed transatlantic service 1919–32. Laid up 1933–34. Scrapped at Dunkirk, 1934.

Franconia

Built by Swan, Hunter & Wigham Richardson Ltd, Newcastle, England, 1911. 18,150 gross tons; 625 feet long; 71 feet wide. Steam quadruple-expansion engines, twin screw. Service speed 17 knots. 2,850 passengers (300 First Class, 350 Second Class, 2,200 Third Class).

Built for Cunard Line, British flag. Liverpool–Queenstown–New York or Boston service. Became a troopship during the First World War. Torpedoed and sunk by a German U-boat off Malta on 4 October 1916; twelve lost.

Frederick VIII

Built by Vulcan Shipyards, Stettin, Germany, 1913. 11,580 gross tons; 544 feet long; 62 feet wide. Steam triple-expansion engines, twin screw. Service speed 17 knots. 1,350 passengers (100 First Class, 300 Second Class, 950 Third Class).

Built for Scandinavian-American Line, Danish flag. Copenhagen–Oslo–New York service. Laid up 1935; scrapped 1936.

George Washington

Built by Vulkan Shipyards, Stettin, Germany, 1909. 25,570 gross tons; 723 feet long; 72 feet wide. Steam quadruple-expansion engines, twin screw. Service speed 18½ knots. 2,679 passengers (568 First Class, 433 Second Class, 452 Third Class, 1,226 Steerage).

Built for North German Lloyd, German flag. Bremerhaven–Southampton–Cherbourg–New York service. Interned at New York at the start of the First World War in August 1914; seized by the

Duilio. (Richard Faber Collection)

Above: Florida. (Peabody Essex Museum)

Opposite: France. (Cronican-Arroyo Collection)

THE SHIPS OF ELLIS ISLAND 55

C^IE G^LE TRANSATLANTIQUE ◆ FRENCH LINE
FRANCE
PARIS ◆ HÂVRE ◆ NEW-YORK

Opposite and right: French Line.

58 THE SHIPS OF ELLIS ISLAND

French Line.

Franconia. (Alex Duncan)

THE SHIPS OF ELLIS ISLAND 59

Frederick VIII. (Peabody Essex Museum)

US government in April 1917 and became troopship USS *George Washington*, US flag. Later assigned to the United States Lines, US flag; began Bremerhaven–Southampton–Cherbourg–New York sailings in 1921. Laid up 1932–40. Refitted as a troopship in 1940 for service during the Second World War; renamed *Catlin* but soon reverted to *George Washington*. Damaged by New York pier fire in 1947. Completely destroyed in a fire at Baltimore 1951; wreckage scrapped.

Germanic/Gul-Djemal

Built by Harland & Wolff Ltd, Belfast, Northern Ireland, 1874. 5,071 gross tons; 468 feet long; 45 feet wide. Compound engines, single screw. Service speed 16 knots. 1,700 passengers (200 First Class, 1,500 Third Class).

Built for White Star Line, British flag. Liverpool–Cobh–New York service. Won transatlantic Blue Ribbon for speed in 1876. Sold to American Line, US flag, in 1904. Southampton–New York service. Sold to Dominion Line, British flag, in 1905; renamed *Ottawa*. Liverpool–Canada service. Sold to Turkish owners, Turkish flag, in 1911; renamed *Gul-Djemal*. Mediterranean and Black Sea services. Torpedoed and sunk by a British submarine off the Turkish coast on 3 May 1915; later salvaged and repaired. Sailed for Ottoman-America Line, also Turkish flag, in 1920–21. Constantinople–New York service. Name altered to *Gulcemal* in 1928. Scrapped in Sicily in 1950 after seventy-six years of service.

Giulio Cesare

Built by Swan, Hunter & Wigham Richardson Ltd, Newcastle, England, 1913–22. 21,848 gross tons; 634 feet long; 76 feet wide. Steam turbines, quadruple screw. Service speed 19 knots. 2,373 passengers (243 First Class, 306 Second Class, 1,824 Third Class).

Built for Navigazione Generale Italiana, Italian flag. Laid down in 1913, but construction halted owing to the First World War. Finally completed in 1922. Genoa–Naples–Palermo–New York service. Genoa–Rio de Janeiro–Buenos Aires service after 1925. Transferred to Italian Line 1932. Italy–South Africa service after 1933. Transferred to Lloyd Triestino, Italian flag, in 1937 and used in Italy–Far East service. Laid up 1940–42. Used as an International Red Cross evacuation ship in 1942. Sunk during Allied air raid on Trieste on 11 September 1944. Wreckage scrapped 1949.

Granite State/President Polk

Built by New York Shipbuilding Corporation, Camden, New Jersey, 1922. 10,553 gross tons; 502 feet long; 62 feet wide. Steam triple-expansion engines, twin screw. Service speed 14 knots. 610 passengers (160 cabin class, 450 Third Class).

Built for United States Lines, US flag. Made one New York–Bremerhaven crossing as the *Granite State* but then renamed *President Polk*. London–Cherbourg–Plymouth–Cobh–New York service. Transferred to Dollar Line, US flag, in 1924. Used on an around-the-world service. Transferred to American President Lines, US flag, in 1938. Renamed *President Taylor* in 1940. Stranded off China on 14 February 1942; wreckage later destroyed by Japanese air attack.

THE SHIPS OF ELLIS ISLAND   61

George Washington. (Alex Duncan)

Germanic. (Peabody Essex Museum)

62   THE SHIPS OF ELLIS ISLAND

THE SHIPS OF ELLIS ISLAND 63

Above: Giulio Cesare. (Alex Duncan)

Opposite: Cesare. (Alex Duncan)

Haverford

Built by John Brown & Company Ltd, Clydebank, Scotland, 1901. 11,635 gross tons; 550 feet long; 59 feet wide. Steam triple-expansion engines, twin screw. Service speed 14 knots. 1,850 passengers (150 Second Class, 1,700 Third Class).

Built for American Line, but under British flag. Southampton/Liverpool–New York service. Later Antwerp–Southampton–New York service for Red Star Line and still later Liverpool–Portland and Liverpool–Philadelphia service for Dominion Line. Used as a troopship during the First World War 1915–17. Torpedoed by a German U-boat off Scotland on 26 June 1917; eleven lost. Repaired but then nearly sunk a second time in the North Atlantic on 17 April 1918. Resumed Liverpool–Philadelphia service in 1919 for White Star Line, British flag. Hamburg–New York service for American Line, British flag, in 1922; afterward reverted to White Star Line. Scrapped in Italy 1925.

Hellig Olav

Built by Alexander Stephen & Sons Ltd, Glasgow, Scotland, 1902. 9,939 gross tons; 515 feet long; 58 feet wide. Steam triple-expansion engines, twin screw. Service speed 16 knots. 1,170 passengers (130 First Class, 140 Second Class, 900 Third Class).

Built for Scandinavian-American Line, Danish flag. Copenhagen–Oslo–New York service. Also made some Hamburg–Southampton–Cherbourg–New York voyages for Royal Mail Lines, but under Danish flag. Laid up 1933–34; scrapped 1934.

Homeric

Built by Schichau Shipyards, Danzig, Germany, 1913–22. 34,351 gross tons; 774 feet long; 82 feet wide. Steam triple-expansion engines, twin screw. Service speed 19 knots. 2,766 passengers (529 First Class, 487 Second Class, 1,750 Third Class).

Launched as *Columbus* for North German Lloyd, German flag, but construction then halted owing to the First World War. Ceded to Britain as reparations in 1919; sold to White Star Line, British flag; renamed *Homeric*. Completed in 1922. Southampton–Cherbourg–New York service. Cruising only 1932–35. Transferred to Cunard-White Star Limited, also British flag, in 1934. Scrapped in Scotland 1936.

Imperator/Berengaria

Built by Bremer-Vulkan Shipyards, Hamburg, Germany, 1913. 52,117 gross tons; 919 feet long; 98 feet wide. Steam turbines, quadruple screw. Service speed 23 knots. 4,594 passengers (908 First Class, 972 Second Class, 942 Third Class, 1,772 Steerage).

Built for Hamburg America Line, German flag. Intended to be called *Europa*, but instead named *Imperator*. Largest ship afloat 1913–14. Hamburg–Southampton–Cherbourg–New York service. Laid up at Hamburg throughout the First World War, 1914–18. Seized by the United States as reparations in 1919; then allocated to Britain in 1920. Resumed sailing as the *Imperator*, but under the British flag. Southampton–Cherbourg–New York service. Sold to Cunard Line, British flag, in 1921; refitted and renamed *Berengaria*. Transferred to Cunard-White Star Limited in 1934. Withdrawn from service 1938; scrapping began in 1939, but final remains not scrapped until 1946.

Haverford. (Alex Duncan)

Hellig Olav. (Alex Duncan)

66 THE SHIPS OF ELLIS ISLAND

Left: *Homeric*. (White Star Line)

Opposite left: Hamburg America Line.

Opposite right: Cunard Line.

Imperator as *Berengaria*. (Alex Duncan)

THE SHIPS OF ELLIS ISLAND 67

Ivernia

Built by Swan, Hunter & Wigham Richardson Ltd, Newcastle, England, 1900. 13,799 gross tons; 600 feet long; 64 feet wide. Steam triple-expansion engines, twin screw. Service speed 15 knots. 1,960 passengers (160 First Class, 200 Second Class, 1,600 Third Class).

Built for Cunard Line, British flag. Liverpool–Cobh–New York service; later Liverpool–Cobh–Boston service and Fiume–Trieste–Venice–Palermo–New York services. Used as a transport ship during the First World War. Torpedoed and sunk by a German U-boat on 1 January 1917; thirty-six lost.

Kaiser Wilhelm II

Built by Vulkan Shipyards, Stettin, Germany, 1903. 19,361 gross tons; 707 feet long; 72 feet wide. Steam quadruple-expansion engines, twin screw. Service speed 23 knots. 1,888 passengers (775 First Class, 343 Second Class, 770 Steerage).

Built for North German Lloyd, German flag. Bremerhaven–Southampton–Cherbourg–New York service. World's fastest ship 1906/07. Laid up at New York at the start of the First World War, August 1914. Seized by the US government in April 1917; became the troopship USS *Agamemnon*. Laid up 1919–40; renamed *Monticello* in 1929. Scrapped at Baltimore 1940.

Kaiser Wilhelm der Grosse

Built by Vulkan Shipyards, Stettin, Germany, 1897. 14,439 gross tons; 655 feet long; 66 feet wide. Steam triple-expansion engines, twin screw. Service speed 22 knots. 1,970 passengers (558 First Class, 338 Second Class, 1,074 Steerage).

Built for North German Lloyd, German flag. World's largest ship 1897/99; world's fastest ship 1897–1900. Bremerhaven–Southampton–Cherbourg–New York service. Became an auxiliary cruiser for the German Navy at the start of the First World War in August 1914 and later sank three Allied ships. Scuttled in Spanish West Africa to avoid capture by the British on 26 August 1914.

Koningin Luise/Edison

Built by Vulkan Shipyards, Stettin, Germany, 1897. 10,566 gross tons; 552 feet long; 60 feet wide. Steam quadruple-expansion engines, twin screw. Service speed 14½ knots. 2,400 passengers (225 First Class, 235 Second Class, 1,940 Steerage).

Built for North German Lloyd, German flag. Bremerhaven–Southampton–Cherbourg service and later Bremerhaven–Australia service. Still later Naples–Genoa–New York service. Laid up throughout the First World War, 1914–18. Ceded to Britain as reparations in 1919 and assigned to the Orient Line, British flag, for London–Melbourne–Sydney service. Purchased outright by Orient Line in 1921 and renamed *Omar*. Sold to Byron Steamship Company, also British, in 1924; renamed *Edison* for Patras–Piraeus–Constantinople–Constanza–New York service. Transferred to Greek flag 1929. Scrapped in Italy 1935.

Kronprinz Wilhelm

Built by Vulkan Shipyards, Stettin, Germany, 1901. 14,908 gross tons; 664 feet long; 66 feet wide. Steam quadruple-expansion engines, twin

THE SHIPS OF ELLIS ISLAND 69

Ivernia. (Alex Duncan)

Kaiser Wilhelm II. (Hapag-Lloyd)

Hapag-Lloyd.

Kaiser Wilhelm II. (Hapag-Lloyd)

72   THE SHIPS OF ELLIS ISLAND

Above: Kaiser Wilhelm der Grosse. (Hapag-Lloyd)

Right: Kaiser Wilhelm der Grosse. (Don Stoltenberg Collection)

Koningin Luise. (Hapag-Lloyd)

Kronprinzessin Cecilie. (Hapag-Lloyd)

Hapag-Lloyd.

screw. Service speed 22 knots. 1,761 passengers (367 First Class, 340 Second Class, 1,054 Steerage).

Built for North German Lloyd, German flag. Bremerhaven–Southampton–Cherbourg–New York service. Refitted as an auxiliary cruiser at the start of the First World War in August 1914; subsequently sank fifteen Allied ships. Interned at Newport News, Virginia, in 1915 and seized in 1917 by the US government; refitted as the troopship USS *Von Steuben*. Laid up 1919; scrapped at Baltimore 1923.

Kronprinzessin Cecilie

Built by Vulkan Shipyards, Stettin, Germany, 1906. 19,360 gross tons; 707 feet long; 72 feet wide. Steam quadruple engines, twin screw. Service speed 23 knots. 1,970 passengers (558 First Class, 338 Second Class, 1,074 Steerage).

Built for North German Lloyd, German flag. Bremerhaven–Southampton–Cherbourg–New York service. Seized by the US government during the First World War, in 1917; outfitted as the transport USS *Mount Vernon*. Laid up 1919–40. Scrapped at Baltimore 1940.

Laconia

Built by Swan, Hunter & Wigham Richardson Ltd, Newcastle-upon-Tyne, England, 1922. 19,860 gross tons; 623 feet long; 73 feet wide. Steam turbines, twin screw. Service speed 16 knots. 2,180 passengers (340 First Class, 340 Second Class, 1,500 Third Class).

Built for Cunard Line, British flag. Liverpool–Cobh–New York service. Became a troopship during the Second World War, in 1940. Torpedoed and sunk by a German submarine in the South Atlantic in September 1942; over 2,500 lost, including 1,800 Italian prisoners of war.

Laurentic

Built by Harland & Wolff Ltd, Belfast, Northern Ireland, 1909. 14,982 gross tons; 565 feet long; 67 feet wide. Steam triple-expansion engines, triple screw. Service speed 17 knots. 1,660 passengers (230 First Class, 430 Second Class, 1,000 Third Class).

Built for White Star Line, British flag. Liverpool–Montreal service; some Liverpool–Queenstown–New York sailings. Mined and sunk off Ireland on 25 January 1917; 350 lost.

Liguria

Built by G. Ansaldo & Company, Sestri Ponente, Italy, 1901. 5,127 gross tons; 403 (bp) feet long; 46 feet wide. Steam triple-expansion engines, single screw. Service speed 14 knots. 1,250 passengers (56 First Class, 1,194 Third Class).

Built for Navigazione Generale Italiana, Italian flag. Genoa–Naples–Messina–New York service. Sold to La Veloce Line, also Italian flag, in 1909. Sold to Russian Steam Navigation Company, Russian flag, in 1911; renamed *Affon*. Scrapped 1928.

Lusitania

Built by John Brown & Company Ltd, Clydebank, Scotland, 1907. 31,550 gross tons; 787 feet long; 87 feet wide. Steam turbines,

Above: *Laconia.* (Alex Duncan)

Left: Hapag-Lloyd.

LACONIA

Above and right: Cunard Line.

78 THE SHIPS OF ELLIS ISLAND

Laurentic. (Alex Duncan)

Liguria. (Peabody-Essex Museum)

Lusitania. (Cunard Line)

GREAT WESTERN RAILWAY
MAURETANIA
G.W.R. TENDERS
FETCH & CARRY
PASSENGERS
Baggage & Mails
PLYMOUTH
FISHGUARD
MEETING THE BIG SHIPS

Opposite and right: Cunard Line.

quadruple screw. Service speed 25 knots. 2,165 passengers (563 First Class, 464 Second Class, 1,138 Third Class).

Built for Cunard Line, British flag. Liverpool–Cobh–New York service. Torpedoed and sunk off the Irish coast on 7 May 1915; 1,198 lost.

Majestic

Built by Blohm & Voss Shipbuilders, Hamburg, Germany, 1914–22. 56,551 gross tons; 950 feet long; 100 feet wide; 35-foot draft. Steam turbines, quadruple screw. Service speed 23½ knots. 2,145 passengers (750 First Class, 545 Second Class, 850 Third Class).

Launched as the *Bismarck* for Hamburg America Line, German flag, but not completed because of the First World War. Idle and incomplete, 1914–19. Ceded to Britain and completion work resumed 1919. Sold to the White Star Line, British flag, 1921 and completed as the *Majestic*. World's largest liner until 1935. Southampton–Cherbourg–New York service. Sold for scrap in 1936 but then resold to British Admiralty and refitted as cadets' training ship HMS *Caledonia*. Burned and sank while moored at Rosyth, Scotland, on 29 September 1939. Scrapped 1940–43.

Mauretania

Built by Swan, Hunter & Wigham Richardson Ltd, Newcastle, England, 1907. 31,938 gross tons; 790 feet long; 88 feet wide. Steam turbines, quadruple screw. Service speed 25 knots. 2,335 passengers (560 First Class, 475 Second Class, 1,300 Third Class).

Built for Cunard Line, British flag. Liverpool–Cobh–New York service. World's fastest liner 1907–29. Wartime service as a troop transport and hospital ship, 1914–18. Used primarily as a cruise ship 1930–34. Broken up in Scotland 1935.

Mount Carroll

Built by Merchant Shipbuilding Corporation, Chester, Pennsylvania, 1921. 7,469 gross tons; 440 (bp) feet long; 57 feet wide. Steam turbines, single screw. Service speed 14 knots. 1,050 all-Third Class passengers.

Built for United American Lines, American flag. Hamburg–Boulogne–Plymouth–New York service. Sold to Matson Line, also American flag, in 1925; renamed *Maunawili*. California–Hawaii service. Sold to Panamanian flag owners in 1946; renamed *Socrates*. Sold to Liberian flag owners in 1955; renamed *Southern Albatross*. Promptly resold to British owners; renamed *Portaritissa*. Scrapped in Japan 1959.

Munchen

Built by Vulkan Works, Stettin, Germany, 1922. 13,483 gross tons; 551 feet long; 65 feet wide. Steam triple-expansion engines, twin screw. Service speed 16 knots. 1,079 passengers (171 First Class, 350 Second Class, 558 Third Class).

Built for North German Lloyd, German flag. Bremerhaven–New York service or Bremerhaven–Boulogne–Cobh–New York service. She burned and sank at her New York pier on 11 February 1930; later refloated and returned to Germany. Repaired and refitted; renamed *General von Steuben*. Renamed *Steuben* in 1938. 1939–45 war service. Torpedoed and sunk in the Baltic Sea by a Soviet submarine on 10 February 1945; over 3,000 lost.

Above: Majestic. (F. W. Hawks)

Right: White Star Line.

Above: Mauretania. (Cronican-Arroyo Collection)

Right: Don Stoltenberg Collection.

Above and right: Cunard Line.

Mount Carroll. (Alex Duncan)

München as *Steuben*. (Hapag-Lloyd)

Nieuw Amsterdam

Built by Harland & Wolff Ltd, Belfast, Northern Ireland, 1906. 16,967 gross tons; 615 feet long; 68 feet wide. Steam quadruple-expansion engines, twin screw. Service speed 16 knots. 2,886 passengers (440 First Class, 246 Second Class, 2,200 Third Class).

Built for Holland America Line, Dutch flag. Rotterdam–Boulogne–Plymouth–New York service. Last major passenger liner to be fitted with auxiliary sails. Scrapped in Japan 1932.

Noordam/Kungsholm

Built by Harland & Wolff Ltd, Belfast, Northern Ireland, 1902. 12,531 gross tons; 575 feet long; 62 feet wide. Steam quadruple engines, twin screw. Service speed 15 knots. 2,278 passengers (286 First Class, 192 Second Class, 1,800 Third Class). Built for Holland America Line, Dutch flag. Rotterdam–Boulogne–Plymouth–New York service. 1917 laid-up after mine damages. Rotterdam–Brest–Falmouth–New York service 1919–23. Chartered to Swedish American Line and renamed *Kungsholm* in 1923. Gothenburg–Copenhagen–New York service. Reverted to Holland America Line and renamed *Noordam* in 1925. Sold in 1927; scrapped 1928.

Oceanic

Built by Harland & Wolff Ltd, Belfast, Northern Ireland, 1899. 17,272 gross tons; 704 feet long; 63 feet wide. Steam triple-expansion engines, twin screw. Service speed 19 knots. 1,710 passengers (410 First Class, 300 Second Class, 1,000 Steerage).

Built for White Star Line, British flag. Liverpool–Queenstown–New York service. World's largest liner 1899–1901. First ship to exceed 700 feet in length. Stranded in the Shetland Islands in September 1914 soon after being converted to a wartime auxiliary cruiser. Total loss and gradually scrapped on the spot until 1924.

Olympic

Built by Harland & Wolff Ltd, Belfast, Northern Ireland, 1911. 45,324 gross tons; 882 feet long; 92 feet wide. Steam triple-expansion engines, triple screw. Service speed 21 knots. 2,764 passengers (1,054 First Class, 510 Second Class, 1,200 Third Class).

Built for White Star Line, British flag. Southampton–Cherbourg–New York service. Largest liner in the world 1911–12. Served as a troopship during the First World War 1914–18. Resumed transatlantic service 1920–34. Transferred to Cunard-White Star Limited in 1934. Laid up 1935. Scheduled to be scrapped in Jarrow, England, but last remains broken up in Scotland 1937.

Orbita

Built by Harland & Wolff Ltd, Belfast, Northern Ireland, 1915. 15,678 gross tons; 568 feet long; 67 feet wide. Steam triple-expansion engines, triple screw. Service speed 14 knots. 887 passengers (190 First Class, 221 Second Class, 476 Third Class).

Built for Pacific Steam Navigation Company Ltd, British flag. Completed for service as a troopship during the First World War, 1915–19. Liverpool–West Coast of South America service 1919–21. Transferred to Royal Mail Lines, also British flag, in 1921; Hamburg–

Southampton–Cherbourg–New York service 1921–27. Resumed South American service 1927–39. Sailed as a troopship 1939–50. Broken in Wales 1950.

Oropesa

Built by Cammell Laird & Company, Birkenhead, England, 1920. 14,072 gross tons; 552 feet long; 66 feet wide. Steam turbines, twin screw. Service speed 14½ knots. 632 passengers (141 First Class, 131 Second Class, 360 Third Class).

Built for Pacific Steam Navigation Company Ltd, British flag. Liverpool–West Coast of South America service 1920–21. Chartered to Royal Mail Lines, also British flag, 1921–22; Hamburg–Southampton–Cherbourg–New York service. Resumed South American service 1922–31. Laid up 1931–37. Resumed South American service 1937–39. Used as a troopship 1939–41. Torpedoed and sunk by a German submarine off Northern Ireland on 16 January 1941; 113 lost.

Oscar II

Built by Alexander Stephen & Sons Ltd, Glasgow, Scotland, 1901. 10,012 gross tons; 515 feet long; 56 feet wide. Steam triple-expansion engines, twin screw. Service speed 16 knots. 1,170 passengers (130 First Class, 140 Second Class, 900 Third Class).

Built for Scandinavian American Line, Danish flag. Copenhagen–Oslo–New York service. Laid up 1931–33. Scrapped in Scotland 1933.

Panhandle State/President Monroe

Built by New York Shipbuilding Corporation, Camden, New Jersey, 1921. 10,553 gross tons; 502 feet long; 62 feet wide. Steam triple-expansion engines, twin screw. Service speed 14 knots. Seventy-eight one-class passengers.

Built for United States Mail Steamship Company, US flag. New York–Plymouth–Cherbourg–London service. Soon transferred to United States Lines, also US flag; renamed *President Monroe* in 1922. Transferred to Dollar Line, also US flag, in 1924 for around-the-world service. Downgraded to a freighter 1938. Renamed *President Buchanan* in 1940. Became US Navy hospital ship in 1943; renamed USS *Emily H. M. Weder*. Reverted to *President Buchanan* in 1945. Laid up 1945–57. Scrapped in California 1957.

Paris (1921)

Built by Chantiers de l'Atlantique, St Nazaire, France, 1913–21. 34,569 gross tons; 764 feet long; 85 feet wide. Steam turbines, quadruple screw. Service speed 22 knots. 1,930 passengers (560 First Class, 530 Second Class, 840 Third Class).

Built for French Line, French flag. Construction began in 1913, but slowed owing to the First World War. Launched 1916, but remained incomplete until 1921. Le Havre–Southampton/Plymouth–New York service. Burned and capsized at Le Havre on 19 April 1939. Wreckage scrapped 1947.

Above: Oceanic. (Alex Duncan)

Right: White Star Line.

Olympic. (Author's Collection)

Orbita. (Michael Cassar Collection)

Oropesa. (Alex Duncan)

Oscar II. (Peabody Essex Museum)

Panhandle Estate. (Alex Duncan)

Paris. (Author's Collection)

French Line.

Patria

Built by Chantiers de la Mediterranee, La Seyne, France, 1913. 11,885 gross tons; 512 feet long; 59 feet wide. Steam triple-expansion engines, twin screw. Service speed 16 knots. 2,240 passengers (140 First Class, 250 Second Class, 1,850 Third Class).

Built for Fabre Line, French flag. Marseilles–New York service (occasionally extended to include Piraeus, Istanbul, Beirut, Jaffa and Alexandria). Transferred to Messageries Martimes, also French flag, 1932–40. Marseilles–Eastern Mediterranean service. Sunk by sabotage explosion in the harbour at Haifa on 25 November 1940. Salvaged and scrapped 1952.

Pittsburgh

Built by Harland & Wolff Ltd, Belfast, Northern Ireland, 1913–22. 16,332 gross tons; 600 feet long; 67 feet wide. Steam triple-expansion engines, triple screw. Service speed 15 knots. 2,400 passengers (600 Cabin Class, 1,800 Third Class).

Laid down in 1913 for the American Line, but under British flag. Construction later halted owing to the First World War. Completed for White Star Line, also British flag, in 1922. Liverpool–Cobh–New York/Boston service; later Hamburg–Southampton–Cherbourg–New York/Boston service. Sold to Red Star Line, also British flag, in 1925; renamed *Pennland* in 1926. Antwerp–Southampton/London–New York service. Placed under German flag 1935. Sold to Holland America Line, Dutch flag, in 1939. British troopship 1940/41. Bombed and sunk by German aircraft in Greek waters in 1941.

President Lincoln

Built by Harland & Wolff Ltd, Belfast, Northern Ireland, 1907. 18,168 gross tons; 616 feet long; 68 feet wide. Steam quadruple-expansion engines, twin screw. Service speed 14½ knots. 3,828 passengers (324 First Class, 152 Second Class, 1,004 Third Class, 2,348 Steerage).

Originally intended to be the *Scotian* for Leyland Line, British flag, but sold before completion to Hamburg America Line, German flag. Intended to be named *Berlin*, but changed to *President Lincoln* prior to completion. Hamburg–Southampton–Boulogne–New York service. Laid up at New York at the start of the First World War in August 1914. Seized by the US government in 1917 and became troopship USS *President Lincoln*, US flag. Sunk in the Atlantic by a German U-boat on 31 May 1918; twenty-six lost.

President Roosevelt

Built by New York Shipbuilding Corporation, Camden, New Jersey, 1922. 13,869 gross tons; 535 feet long; 72 feet wide. Steam turbines, twin screw. Service speed 18 knots. 644 passengers (320 First Class, 324 Third Class).

Built as *Peninsular State* for United States Lines, US flag. Tentatively renamed *President Pierce*, but promptly renamed *President Roosevelt*. New York–Plymouth/Southampton–Le Havre–Hamburg service. Became US government troopship during the Second World War in 1940 and renamed USS *Joseph T. Dickman*. Scrapped in California, 1948.

THE SHIPS OF ELLIS ISLAND   95

Above and right: President Lincoln. (Hapag-Lloyd)

96   THE SHIPS OF ELLIS ISLAND

President Roosevelt. (Alex Duncan)

Prinz Eitel Friedrich/Mount Clay

Built by A. G. Vulcan Shipyard, Stettin, Germany, 1904. 8,865 gross tons; 488 (bp) feet long; 55 feet wide. Steam quadruple-expansion engines. Service speed 15 knots. 1,306 passengers (six Cabin Class, 1,300 Third Class).

Built for North German Lloyd, German flag. Hamburg–New York service. Laid up during the First World War, 1916–17. Seized by US government in 1917 and became US flag troopship USS *De Kalb*. Transferred to United American Lines, US flag, in 1920; renamed *Mount Clay*. Hamburg–Southampton–Cherbourg–New York service 1920–25. Laid up 1925–34. Scrapped 1934.

Providence

Built by Forges et Chantiers de la Mediterranee, La Seyne, France, 1915. 11,996 gross tons; 511 feet long; 59 feet wide. Steam triple-expansion engines, twin screw. Service speed 16 knots. 2,240 passengers (140 First Class, 250 Second Class, 1,850 Third Class).

Built for Fabre Line, French flag. Marseilles–New York (occasionally extended to include Piraeus, Istanbul, Beirut, Jaffa and Alexandria) service. Transferred to Messageries Maritmes, also French flag, 1932. Scrapped in Italy 1951.

Randsfjord

Built by North Eastern Marine Engineering Co. Ltd, Sunderland, England, 1914. 3,222 gross tons; 339 (bp) feet long; 48 feet wide. Steam triple-expansion engines, single screw. Service speed 12 knots. Up to twelve Cabin Class passengers, but temporary Third Class quarters for as many as 500 arranged.

Built by Kongfors for T. Thoresen, Norwegian flag. Sold to Norwegian America Line, also Norwegian flag, in 1921 and renamed *Randsfjord*. Oslo–Kristianand–Stavanger–Bergen–Copenhagen–New York sailings. Sold to Finnish owners, Finnish flag, in 1934; renamed *Gertrud*. Sold to other Finnish owners in 1938; renamed *Wilja*. Torpedoed and sunk by a German submarine off the English coast on 17 February 1940.

Reliance

Built by J. C. Tecklenberg Shipyard, Geestemunde, Germany, 1920. 19,582 gross tons; 615 feet long; 71 feet wide. Steam triple-expansion engines, triple screw. Service speed 16 knots. 1,010 passengers (290 First Class, 320 Second Class, 400 Third Class).

Launched in 1914 as *Johann Heinrich Burchard* for Hamburg America Line, German flag, but remained idle and incomplete during the First World War. Sold to Royal Holland Lloyd, Dutch flag, in 1916; renamed *Limburgia*. Completed in 1920 for Amsterdam–East Coast of South America service. Sold to United American Lines, Panamanian flag, in 1922; renamed *Reliance*. Hamburg–Southampton–Cherbourg–New York service. Sold to Hamburg America Line, German flag, in 1926. Thereafter used primarily as a cruise ship. Caught fire and burned at Hamburg on 7 August 1938; wreckage scrapped 1941.

Resolute

Built by A. G. Weser Shipbuilders, Bremen, Germany, 1914–20. 20,200 gross tons; 616 feet long; 72 feet wide. Steam triple-expansion engines, triple screw. Service speed 16 knots. 1,945 passengers (335 First Class, 284 Second Class, 469 Third Class, 857 Steerage).

Launched in 1914 as *William O'Swald* for Hamburg America Line, German flag, but remained incomplete due to the First World War. Sold to Royal Holland Lloyd, Dutch flag, in 1916; renamed *Brabantia* and completed in 1920. Amsterdam–East Coast of South America service. Sold to United American Lines, Panamanian flag, in 1922; renamed *Resolute*. Hamburg–Southampton–Cherbourg–New York service. Purchased by Hamburg America Line, German flag, in 1926. Cruising only after 1928. Sold to the Italian government, Italian flag, in 1935; renamed *Lombardia*. Used for passenger and troopship services. Bombed, burned out and sank in Allied air raid on Naples on 4 August 1943. Wreckage raised and scrapped at La Spezia 1946.

Rijndam

Built by Harland & Wolff Ltd, Belfast, Northern Ireland, 1901. 12,527 gross tons; 575 feet long; 62 feet wide. Steam triple-expansion engines, twin screw. Service speed 15 knots. 2,282 passengers (286 First Class, 196 Second Class, 1,800 Steerage).

Built for Holland America Line, Dutch flag. Rotterdam–Boulogne–New York service. Laid up in 1917 owing to the First World War; used as a US Navy troopship during 1918. Resumed Rotterdam–Boulogne–Plymouth–New York service 1919–28. Scrapped in Holland 1929.

Rotterdam

Built by Harland & Wolff Ltd, Belfast, Northern Ireland, 1908. 24,149 gross tons; 667 feet long; 77 feet wide. Steam quadruple-expansion engines, twin screw. Service speed 17 knots. 3,575 passengers (520 First Class, 555 Second Class, 2,500 Third Class).

Built for Holland America Line, Dutch flag. Rotterdam–Boulogne–Plymouth–New York service. Laid up for most of the First World War, 1914–18. Resumed passenger service 1919; scrapped in Holland, 1940.

Russia/Latvia

Built by Barclay Curle & Co. Ltd, Glasgow, Scotland, 1908. 8,596 gross tons; 475 (bp) feet long; 57 feet wide. Steam triple-expansion engines, twin screw. Service speed 16 knots. Exact information lacking on passenger capacity.

Built for Russian American Line, Russian flag. Libau–Danzig–New York service. Laid up at Kronstadt, Russia, in August 1914 owing to the First World War. Later resumed sailing but for other Russian owners; renamed *Rossija* in 1917 and later renamed *Russ*. Sold to Baltic American Line, Danish flag, in 1921; renamed *Latvia*. Libau–Hamburg/Copenhagen–New York service. Sold to Osaka Shosen Kaisha, Japanese flag, in 1924; renamed *Fuso Maru* and later *Huso Maru*. Lost during the Second World War.

THE SHIPS OF ELLIS ISLAND 99

Mount Clay. (Alex Duncan)

Randsfjord. (Alex Duncan)

100 THE SHIPS OF ELLIS ISLAND

Reliance. (Hapag-Lloyd)

Resolute. (F. W. Hawks)

THE SHIPS OF ELLIS ISLAND 101

Hapag-Lloyd.

102 THE SHIPS OF ELLIS ISLAND

Rijndam. (Duncan Haws)

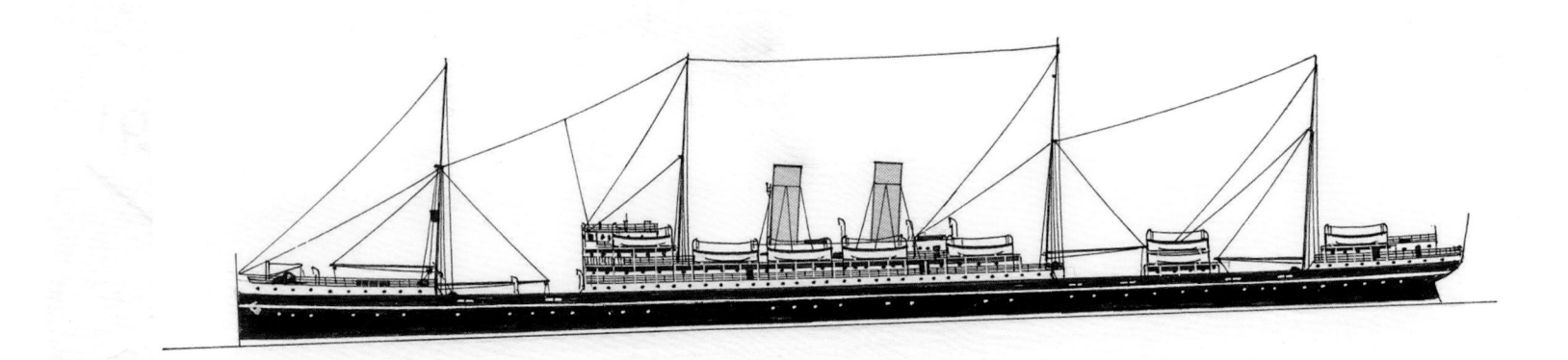

Russia. (Duncan Haws)

St Louis

Built by William Cramp Shipbuilders, Philadelphia, Pennsylvania, 1895. 11,629 gross tons; 554 feet long; 63 feet wide. Steam quadruple-expansion engines, twin screw. Service speed 19 knots. 1,340 passengers (320 First Class, 220 Second Class, 800 Steerage).

Built for American Line, US flag. Southampton/Liverpool–New York service. Used by the US Navy as an auxiliary cruiser during the Spanish–American War of 1898. Afterwards, resumed transatlantic service. Used as an armed merchant transport by the US Navy during the First World War, 1917–20; renamed USS *Louisville*. Reverted to the American Line in 1920, renamed *St Louis*, but badly damaged by fire while being restored as a passenger ship. Laid up 1920–24. There were plans to rebuild her as a cruise ship in 1922, which never materialized; scrapped at Genoa 1924.

Samaria

Built by Cammell Laird & Co. Ltd, Birkenhead, England, 1921. 19,602 gross tons; 624 feet long; 73 feet wide. Steam turbines, twin screw. Service speed 16 knots. 2,190 passengers (350 First Class, 340 Second Class, 1,500 Third Class).

Built for Cunard Line, British flag. Liverpool–Cobh–New York/Boston/Montreal service. Used as a troopship during the Second World War, 1939–47. Liverpool–Montreal service 1950–55. Scrapped in Scotland, 1956.

San Giorgio

Built by Oswald Mordaunt & Company, Southampton, England, 1886. 2,817 gross tons; 307 (bp) feet long; 41 feet wide. Compound engines, single screw. Service speed 11 knots. 920 passengers (20 First Class, 900 Third Class).

Intended to be named *Shakespeare* for British owners, but completed instead as *San Giorgio* for Italian owners, Italian flag. Transferred to Navigazione Generale Italiana, also Italian flag, in 1892. Genoa–Naples–Messina–New York service. Sold to other Italian owners in 1910. Wrecked off Italy on 23 November 1920.

San Guglielmo

Built by D. & W. Henderson & Company, Glasgow, Scotland, 1911. 8,341 gross tons; 470 (bp) feet long; 56 feet wide. Steam triple-expansion engines, twin screw. Service speed 15½ knots. 2,425 passengers (50 First Class, 175 Second Class, 2,200 Third Class).

Built for Sicula Americana Lines, Italian flag. Messina–Palermo–Naples–New York service. Also later sailed for Transoceanica Line, also Italian flag. Torpedoed and sunk by a German U-boat off Italy on 8 January 1918.

Sant' Anna

Built by Forges et Chantiers de la Mediterranee, La Seyne, France, 1910. 9,350 gross tons; 470 (bp) feet long; 56 feet wide. Steam triple-expansion engines, twin screw. Service speed 16 knots. 1,970 passengers (70 First Class, 150 Second Class, 1,750 Third Class).

Built for Fabre Line, French flag. Marseilles–New York (occasionally extended to include Piraeus, Istanbul, Beirut, Jaffa and Alexandria) service. Torpedoed and sunk by a German U-boat off North Africa on 11 May 1918.

Saxonia

Built by John Brown & Co. Ltd, Clydebank, Scotland, 1900. 14,917 gross tons; 600 feet long; 64 feet wide. Steam quadruple-expansion engines, twin screw. Service speed 16 knots. 1,960 passengers (160 First Class, 200 Second Class, 1,600 Third Class).

Built for Cunard Line, British flag. Liverpool–Queenstown–Boston service and later Fiume–Trieste–Venice–Palermo–Boston service. Used during the First World War by the British government as a troopship and later as a prisoners-of-war accommodation center, 1914–18. Liverpool–Queenstown–New York service beginning in 1919 and later Hamburg–Southampton–Cherbourg–New York service. Scrapped in Holland, 1925.

Scythia

Built by Vickers-Armstrong Shipbuilders Ltd, Barrow-in-Furness, England, 1921. 19,730 gross tons; 624 feet long; 73 feet wide. Steam turbines, twin screw. Service speed 16 knots. 2,206 passengers (337 First Class, 331 Second Class, 1,538 Third Class).

Built for Cunard Line, British flag. Liverpool–Queenstown–New York service. Used as a troopship during the Second World War, 1939–48. Liverpool–Cobh–Montreal service 1950–57. Scrapped in Scotland, 1958.

Stavangerfjord

Built by Cammell Laird & Company, Birkenhead, England, 1918. 13,156 gross tons; 553 feet long; 64 feet wide. Steam quadruple-expansion engines, twin screw. Service speed 16 knots. 1,206 passengers (88 First Class, 318 Second Class, 820 Third Class).

Built for Norwegian America Line, Norwegian flag. Oslo–Bergen–Kristiansand–Copenhagen–New York service. Laid up during the Second World War, 1939–45. Resumed service 1945–63. Scrapped in Hong Kong, 1963.

Taormina

Built by D. & W. Henderson Ltd, Glasgow, Scotland, 1912. 8,282 gross tons; 520 feet long; 58 feet wide. Steam triple-expansion engines, twin screw. Service speed 16½ knots. 2,680 passengers (60 First Class, 120 Second Class, 2,500 Third Class).

Intended for the Henderson Line, British flag, but sold prior to completion to Lloyd Italiano, Italian flag. Genoa–Naples–New York service. Transferred to Navigazione Generale Italiana, also Italian flag, in 1918. Scrapped in Italy, 1929.

Transylvania

Built by Scott's Shipbuilding & Engineering Co., Greenock, Scotland, 1914. 14,315 gross tons; 565 feet long; 66 feet wide. Steam turbines, twin screw. Service speed 16 knots. 2,420 passengers (270 First Class, 250 Second Class, 1,900 Third Class).

St Louis. (Author's Collection)

Scythia. (Cunard Line)

Cunard Line.

San Giorgio. (Alex Duncan)

San Guglielmo. (Peabody Essex Museum)

Sant' Anna. (Alex Duncan)

THE SHIPS OF ELLIS ISLAND 109

Saxonia. (Alex Duncan)

Above and *opposite:* Cunard Line.

THE SHIPS OF ELLIS ISLAND 111

Stavangerfjord. (Author's Collection)

Taormina. (Alex Duncan)

Built for Cunard Line, British flag, but transferred to Anchor Line, also British flag, in 1915. Liverpool–Queenstown–New York service. Used during the First World War as a troopship, 1915–17. Torpedoed and sunk by a German U-boat off Italy on 4 May 1917; 414 lost.

Tuscania

Built by Alexander Stephen & Sons Ltd, Glasgow, Scotland, 1915. 14,348 gross tons; 567 feet long; 66 feet wide. Steam turbines, twin screw. Service speed 17 knots. 2,417 passengers (271 First Class, 246 Second Class, 1,900 Third Class).

Built for Anchor Line, British flag. Operated jointly with Cunard Line. Glasgow–Londonderry–New York service. Torpedoed and sunk by a German submarine off Northern Ireland on 5 February 1918; 210 lost.

Tyrrhenia/Lancastria

Built by William Beardmore & Co. Ltd, Glasgow, Scotland, 1922. 16,243 gross tons; 578 feet long; 70 feet wide. Steam turbines, twin screw. Service speed 16 knots. 1,785 passengers (265 First Class, 370 Second Class, 1,150 Third Class).

Built for Anchor Line, British flag, but operated by Cunard Line, also British flag. Glasgow–Londonderry–New York/Montreal service; later Hamburg–Southampton–Cherbourg–New York service. Renamed *Lancastria* in 1924. Used for cruising 1932–39. Became a troopship in 1940. Attacked by German bombers at St Nazaire on 17 June 1940; sank within 20 minutes with nearly 5,000 lost.

United States

Built by Alexander Stephen & Sons Ltd, Glasgow, Scotland, 1903. 10,095 gross tons; 515 feet long; 58 feet wide. Steam triple-expansion engines, twin screw. Service speed 16 knots. 1,670 passengers (130 First Class, 140 Second Class, 1,400 Third Class).

Built for Scandinavian-American Line, Danish flag. Copenhagen–Oslo–New York service. Laid up 1934. Damaged by fire at Copenhagen on 2 September 1935; later scrapped in Italy.

Vasari

Built by Sir Raylton Dixon & Co., Middlesbrough, England, 1909. 10,117 gross tons; 486 (bp) feet long; 59 feet wide. Steam quadruple-expansion engines, single screw. Service speed 14 knots. 326 passengers (200 First Class, 48 Second Class, 70 Third Class).

Built for Lamport & Holt Line, British flag. New York–East Coast of South America service. Later Liverpool–Queenstown–New York service for Cunard Line, 1919–21. Resumed South American service 1921–28. Sold to other British owners in 1928 and renamed *Arctic Queen*. Sold to Soviet Union, Soviet flag, in 1935 and renamed *Pischevaia Industria*. No longer listed as sailing by 1960.

Vaterland/Leviathan

Built by Blohm & Voss Shipbuilders, Hamburg, Germany, 1914. 54,282 gross tons; 950 feet long; 100 feet wide. Steam turbines, quadruple screw. Service speed 23 knots. 3,909 passengers (752 First Class, 535 Second Class, 850 Third Class, 1,772 Steerage).

114 THE SHIPS OF ELLIS ISLAND

Transylvania. (Cunard Line)

Tuscania. (World Ship Society)

116   THE SHIPS OF ELLIS ISLAND

Tyrrhenia as *Lancastria*. (Cunard Line)

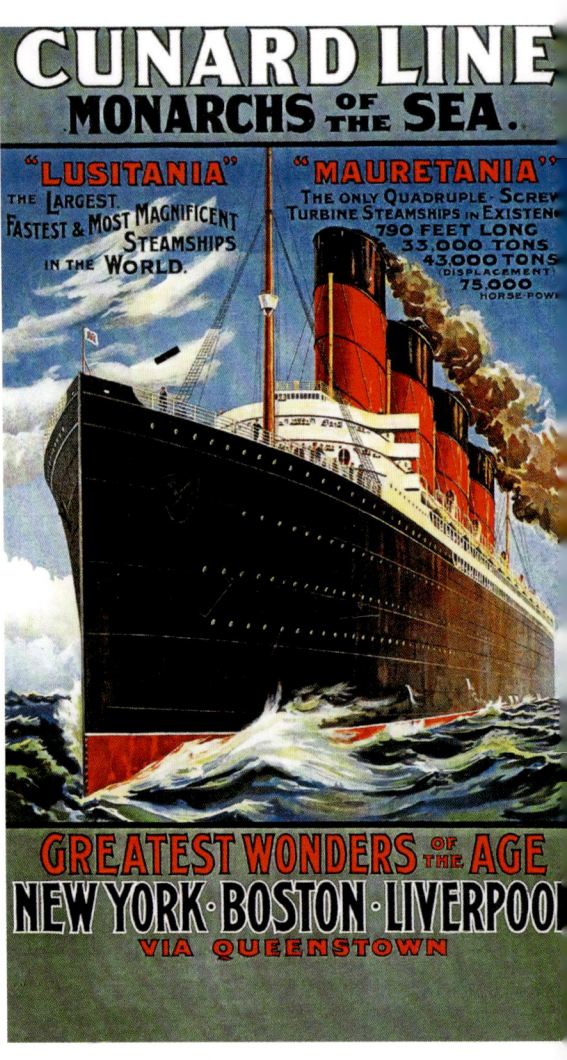

United States. (Alex Duncan)

Vasari. (Alex Duncan)

Built for Hamburg America Line, German flag. Largest liner in the world 1914–21. Hamburg–Southampton–Cherbourg–New York service. Interned at New York at the beginning of the First World War in August 1914. Seized by US government in 1917, US flag; became troopship USS *Leviathan*. Laid up 1919–21. Restored and refitted as a passenger ship 1922/23; thereafter sailed as *Leviathan* for United States Lines, US flag. New York–Cherbourg–Southampton service. Laid up 1932–34. Briefly resumed sailing in 1934 but then laid up thereafter. Scrapped in Scotland, 1938.

Vauban

Built by Workman, Clark & Co. Ltd, Belfast, Northern Ireland, 1912. 10,660 gross tons; 511 feet long; 60 feet wide. Steam quadruple-expansion engines, twin screw. Service speed 13½ knots. 610 passengers (280 First Class, 130 Second Class, 200 Third Class).

Built for Lamport & Holt Line, British flag. New York–East Coast of South America service. Briefly renamed *Alcala* for Royal Mail Lines, also British flag, in 1913 but then reverted to Lamport & Holt Line. Used for Liverpool–Queenstown–New York service 1919–21 for Cunard Line, also British flag. Hamburg–Southampton–Cherbourg–New York service for Royal Mail Lines, also British flag, in 1922. Resumed South American service for Lamport & Holt Lines 1922–32. Scrapped in Scotland, 1932.

Veendam

Built by Harland & Wolff Ltd, Govan, Scotland, 1923. 15,450 gross tons; 579 feet long; 67 feet wide. Steam turbines, twin screw. Service speed 15 knots. 1,898 passengers (262 First Class, 436 Second Class, 1,200 Third Class).

Built for Holland America Line, Dutch flag. Rotterdam–Boulogne–Plymouth–New York service. Damaged by fire during German invasion of Holland in May 1940; later taken to Hamburg by the Germans and used in wartime service. At the end of the war in May 1945, it was found in poor condition. Later repaired and restored in Holland. Resumed Rotterdam–Le Havre–Southampton–New York service 1947–53. Scrapped at Baltimore 1953.

Verona

Built by Workman, Clark & Co. Ltd, Belfast, Northern Ireland, 1907. 8,240 gross tons; 482 (bp) feet long; 58 feet wide. Steam triple-expansion engines, twin screw. Service speed 16 knots. 2,560 passengers (60 First Class, 2,500 Third Class).

Built for Italia Line (Italia Societa Navigazione a Vapore), Italian flag. Naples–Genoa–New York service. Transferred to Navigazione Generale Italiana, also Italian flag, in 1913. Torpedoed and sunk by a German U-boat off Italy on 11 May 1918.

Volendam

Built by Harland & Wolff Limited, Govan, Scotland, 1922. 15,434 gross tons; 572 feet long; 67 feet wide. Steam turbines, twin screw. Service speed 15 knots. 1,899 passengers (263 First Class, 436 Second Class, 1,200 Third Class).

Built for Holland America Line, Dutch flag. Rotterdam–Boulogne–Plymouth–New York service. Troopship service 1940–45. Post-war use as a troopship and passenger ship until 1951. Scrapped in Holland, 1952.

THE SHIPS OF ELLIS ISLAND 119

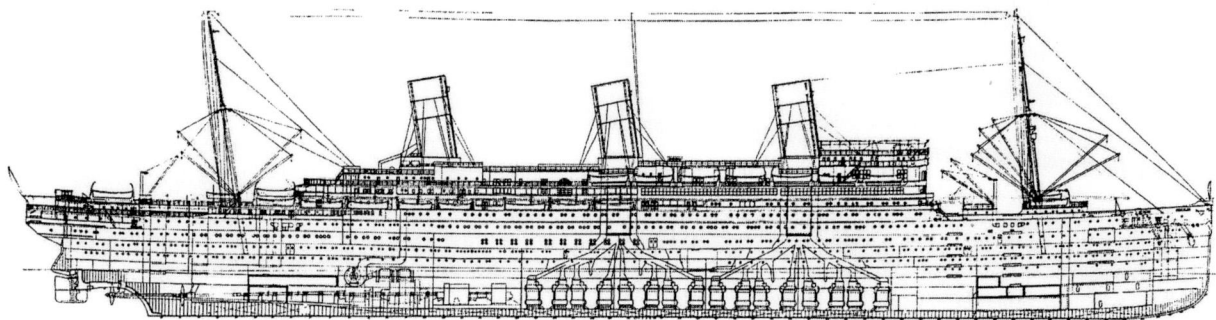

Vaterland. (Hapag-Lloyd)

Vaterland as *Leviathan*. (Alex Duncan)

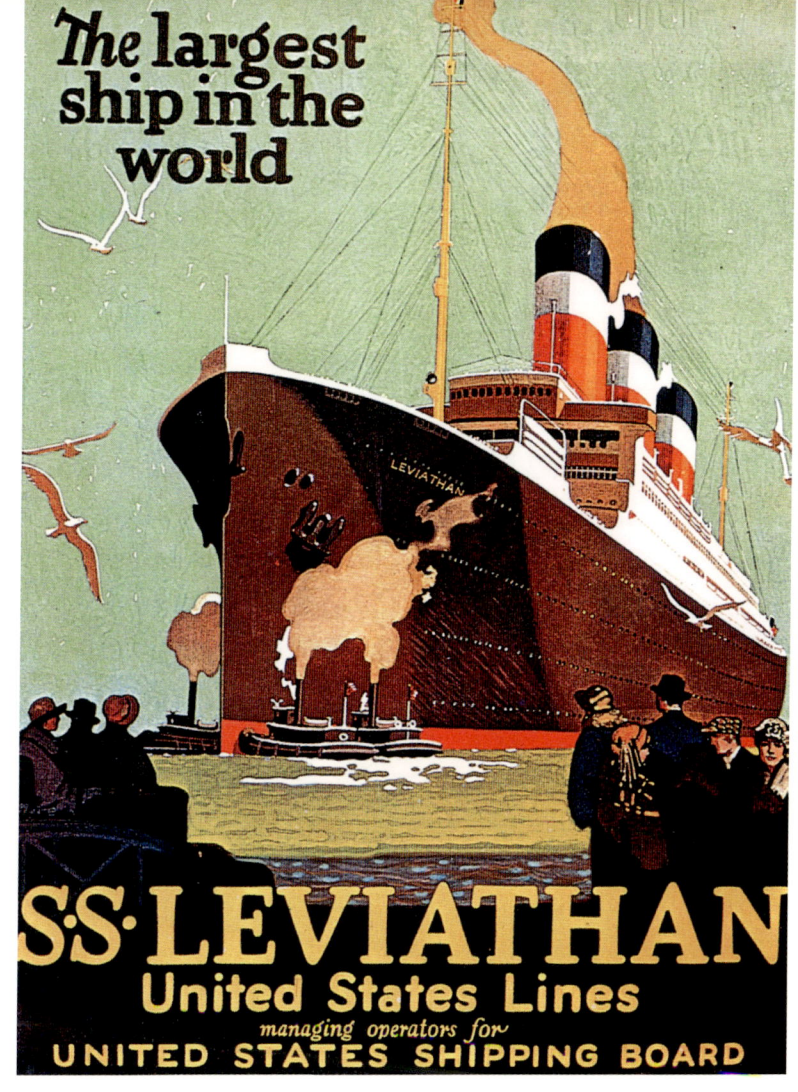

United States Lines.

Author's Collection.

Vauban. (Alex Duncan)

Top and bottom: Veendam.
(Holland America Line)

Verona. (Peabody Essex Museum)

Volendam. (Holland America Line)

Ypiringa/Assyria

Built by Germania Werft (Krupp), Kiel, Germany, 1908. 8,072 gross tons; 449 (bp) feet long; 54 feet wide. Steam quadruple-expansion engines, twin screw. Service speed 13½ knots. 1,260 passengers (100 First Class, 1,160 Third Class).

Built for Hamburg America Line, German flag. Hamburg–West Indies service but also some Hamburg–New York sailings. Laid up during the First World War, 1914–19. Surrendered to Britain in 1919. Sold to Anchor Line, British flag; renamed *Assyria*. Liverpool–Suez–Bombay service and later Glasgow–Londonderry–New York service. Sold to Companhia Colonial, Portugese flag, in 1929; renamed *Colonial*. Lisbon–Africa service. Wrecked in Scotland on 17 September 1950 while en route to the shipbreakers.

Ypiringa. (Peabody Essex Museum)

BIBLIOGRAPHY

Anuta, Michael J., *Ships of Our Ancestors* (Michigan: Genealogical Publishing Co., 1983).

Bonsor, N. R. P., *North Atlantic Seaway* (Preston: T. Stephenson & Sons Ltd, 1955).

Bonsor, N. R. P., *South Atlantic Seaway* (Jersey: Brookside Publications, 1983).

Gibbs, Vernon C. R., *British Passenger Liners of the Five Oceans* (London: Putnam & Company, 1963).

Haws, Duncan, *Merchant Fleets*, Series 1–37 (Pembroke: TCL Publications).

Kludas, Arnold, *Great Passenger Ships of the World*, Vols 1–6 (Cambridge: Patrick Stephens Ltd, 1972–76).

Miller, William H., *Pictorial Encyclopedia of Ocean Liners 1860–1994* (New York: Dover Publications Inc., 1995).

Rabson, Stephen and Kevin O'Donoghue, *P&O: A Fleet History* (Kendal: World Ship Society, 1988).

Smith, Eugene W., *Passenger Ships of the World: Past & Present* (Boston: George H. Dean & Company, 1963).